MODERN CURRICULUM PRESS

POETRY WORKS!
The First Verse

Idea Book

by Babs Bell Hajdusiewicz

MODERN CURRICULUM PRESS
13900 Prospect Road, Cleveland, Ohio 44136
Simon & Schuster • A Paramount Communications Company

MODERN CURRICULUM PRESS
13900 Prospect Road, Cleveland, Ohio 44136
Simon & Schuster • A Paramount Communications Company

ISBN 0-8136-0720-5

1 2 3 4 5 6 7 8 9 10   96 95 94 93 92

CONTENTS

CONTENTS

FOREWORD

Five-year-old Tommy appeared to be practicing what he claimed he would one day be able to do – scale walls like Spiderman. But what was he saying as he leaped in the air? His mother, listening more closely, heard it clearly this time: "When icicles hang by the wall..." She questioned Tommy, who knowingly replied, "That's a poem by Shakespeare, Mommy. Look! I got the icicle. Want a lick?" Here was proof that poetry works!

Poetry in the Classroom

Poetry works in the classroom when the words of poems are meaningful and useful to young children, when words and sounds are interesting, informative, humorous, adventurous, or thought provoking.

Poetry works when we introduce poems we enjoy. Young children listen. They listen because they want to share the experience, to learn, to laugh, to think, and to read, recite, and write those words with us. In short, because of our enjoyment and modeling, children develop their listening, speaking, reading, and writing skills as they strive to make poems their own.

We know poetry works in the classroom when young children make meaningful connections, using the words they've learned to express the images, feelings, and wonder of living. . .

"Mrs. Hajdusiewicz! Look! The fog comes on little cat feet!" My tension from the long drive to school in foggy morning traffic vanished as the four of us stood huddled under the overhang, looking through Carl Sandburg's eyes, singing the poet's words that were now our own. Yes, indeed, poetry works!

A Late Start

Ironically, *Poetry Works! The First Verse* probably had its beginning long ago in a four-room schoolhouse in Burrows, Indiana. Though I loved every other aspect of school, I hated poetry. During my eight years there, I held fast to a dislike of anything resembling a poem, except for Joyce Kilmer's "Trees" because it made sense. A tree was, indeed, lovelier than a poem—or so I believed until my students changed my thinking.

My interest in poetry began with a spontaneous recitation of "Trees," as my sixth graders gathered around to observe a particularly colorful tree in the schoolyard. To my amazement (and theirs, no doubt), they listened in silence—even Randy and Jeremy, who heretofore had little interest in anything but spitballs.

My thinking was challenged again the next year while teaching preadolescents with primary-grade abilities. Early in the year, I noted the children's lack of familiarity with nursery rhymes, so I read aloud and recited a few rhymes. My students were fascinated and wanted more.

Having exhausted my repertoire, I scrambled for more poems. I read every children's poem I could find. Here was an opportunity to grow with my students and, hopefully, assure that they didn't miss what I had.

Every few days we read and reread another of my "finds," throwing out a few but adding most of the poems to our list of favorites to enjoy in some way every day. As the list grew, so did my students' language skills. *And* their self-confidence flowered.

Convinced that poetry was a valuable tool for teaching children of all ages and abilities, I began holding weekly poetry classes for children aged two through six. They came in numbers and brought their friends! These language-loving children couldn't seem to get enough of poetry! As six-year-old "graduates" begged to "keep coming to poetry" and their older siblings kept asking to "just sit in," Pee Wee Poetry™ grew to be a year-round program serving thousands of preschoolers and primary and intermediate children.

Just as my students introduced me to the joys of reading and using poetry, they also led me to writing. Watching their interests, their imaginations, and their needs, I wrote and shared, continually encouraged by their responses and by the conviction that poetry works!

Writing Poetry Works!
The First Verse

Selecting poems for this collection has been fun and rewarding. Fun because in spite of having read and recited the final selections thousands of times, I never tire of their words. I never read one of them without finding some new aspect .

During those thousands of recitations, I have had the pleasure of sharing in children's enthusiasm for poetry—a lit up face, a wiggly giggle, a silent expression of wonderment, or a spontaneous "Do it again!" I know your children will love these poems, and I am equally confident that you, too, will enjoy sharing special moments with poetry in your classroom.

Babs Bell Hajdusiewicz

5

Using *Poetry Works! The First Verse*

Poetry Works! The First Verse will help you enrich your curriculum, using poems that have proven to be popular with young children in classrooms across the country. Its aim is to engage you and your children in enjoyment of meaningful rhythm and rhyme all year long.

Using the Poetry Posters

The collection features fifty-nine Poetry Posters, grouped by theme. Six posters are printless, with each corresponding poem printed on the back, providing additional flexibility for stimulating discussion and storytelling. The Poetry Posters are an ideal way to introduce the poems. Colorful and easy to read, they can be used in small groups or with an entire class.

- Facilitate shared language experiences.
- Use the storage box easel when you introduce or review a poem. Or display Poetry Posters in classroom activity centers: Dress Up Area-"Dressing Up," Clay Center-"I love," Reading Center-"New Baby," Block Area-"from A House is a House for Me," Sand Table- "Sand," Painting-"Rainbow Colors," Science Center-"Beehive" or "Satellite," Store or Cooking Area-"Shopping Day."
- Laminate the posters and write on them with non-permanent markers.
- Provide practice in cloze procedures by masking words and phrases and challenging children to supply them as you read.
- Display groups of posters so children can compare the print and illustrations. Help children identify the pictures that are photos and those created by illustrators.
- Use the posters as models for children's art and writing.
- Use a hole punch and metal rings to "bind" the posters. Create one big "book" or group several posters around a theme.

Using the Idea Book

The Idea Book includes language-development and hands-on activities that will intrigue your children. Its flexible format acknowledges the diversity of classroom organization and teaching styles. Watch for these features:

Responding to the Collection includes teaching suggestions that are specific to the Poster Poems and Theme Openers in the core collection. They will help you involve young children in purposeful talk around a variety of subject areas. The activities include references to the additional poems and songs in the Related Read-Aloud Anthology. Choose the activities that best suit your children's needs and your teaching style. You'll want to use ideas over and over, adapt the suggestions for other poems, and jot your own ideas in the margins as you use the various poems.

Theme Openers stimulate interest in rhythmic language or a particular theme. Reproducible activity pages accompany each poem and provide interactive poem-related experiences in the classroom and at home.

Printless Poetry Posters , with their poems on the back of the poster, offer opportunities for language development through discussion and storytelling. Model writing the words, ideas, and stories children offer as they tell about the illustrations.

Blackline Masters of each Poster Poem and Theme Opener may be reproduced. These masters, which appear opposite the ideas for responding to each poem, have many uses.

- Cut apart the text of a poem. Tape lines or phrases to sheets of drawing paper and invite children to illustrate them.
- Make a transparency and display it on an overhead projector.
- Provide children with copies of favorite poems to illustrate and compile in a book.

Adding Music includes reproducible song pages for several poems. Children will enjoy adding a tune to sing a familiar poem's words, and the music emphasizes the close relationship between poetry and songs.

- Compile songs to make individual song books. Add other favorites.
- Sing a song. Then take away the music and say the poem, or have children say the words as you write them.

Meet the Poets includes pictures of selected poets accompanied by brief biographies. These reproducible pages will help children associate poems with the men and women of yesterday and today who have written poetry to share their thoughts with others.

- Laminate the pictures for display with the corresponding Poetry Posters.
- Illustrate a homophone for "poetry" with a "Poet

Tree."
- Insert poet pictures in anthologies of favorite poems compiled by children.
- Display the Anonymous poet frame with a poem by an anonymous poet. Children can also draw their own pictures in the empty frame when they innovate on poems or create their own.

Related Read-Aloud Anthology will further enrich children's enjoyment of poetry. All of these poems and songs are referenced in the Indexes at the back of the book.

Patterns provide ease in making hand and finger puppets, puzzles, and mobiles.

Indexes help you locate any one of the poems and more than 550 accompanying activities. At the back of the Idea Book, you will find Author; First Line; Title; Curriculum Connections; Family Involvement Activities; Alternate Themes; and Literature, Art, and Music Connections Indexes. The Index of Related Literature, Art, and Music Connections at the end of each unit makes preparation easy.

Using the Cassettes

The four cassettes provide enjoyable listening while presenting poems and songs as models for reciting, reading, and singing. Use the cassettes to introduce or review a poem or for independent listening.

Responding to the Collection

Making Time for Poetry There's never enough time, is there? But aren't you always looking for creative ways to capture and maintain children's interest? Try the following ideas to help you do just that while integrating the rhythm and rhyme of poetry into your busy days with children.
- Introduce a theme or special event with a poem. Read "Rides" or sing "Glug! Gurgle! Glug!" to stimulate interest in an energy or transportation theme. Share "Here Comes the Band" or "Elephant" before a parade.
- Set aside one read-aloud time per week for poetry. Establishing a regular time for poetry helps build a repertoire of familiar poems and sets the stage for the activities for each poem.
- Read or recite one familiar poem every day, or invite children to recite their favorites. Many children will, of course, memorize parts of poems as they recite them again and again.
- Tape record favorite verses so children can listen to them independently.

- Recite or sing poems during those odd moments when children are regrouping or waiting to go home.

Enjoying Nursery Rhymes Nursery rhymes acquaint children with basic vocabulary and provide them with knowledge of the world, two vital prerequisites for reading success. The rhymes are fun to learn and chant out loud. They also lend themselves to dramatization, which encourages children to use their new vocabulary and knowledge naturally. Many children are already familiar with the rhymes and—with a little refresher—so are their families. Nursery rhymes provide an opportunity for children and family members to enjoy poetry together.

Children enjoy reciting and singing the rhymes as they "ride" on a "Nursery Rhyme Train," made by attaching the nursery rhyme posters to the sides of large cardboard boxes.

Reading Aloud Poems are meant to be read aloud. Children love listening as you read and soon want to join in.
- Display the Poetry Poster where children can see it easily. Vary your routine by reciting a poem before introducing the poster, displaying a poster a day or two before reading the poem, or by reading the poem aloud from the Idea Book.
- Introduce the poem by presenting the title and author and then thanking the author: "'I love' by Eloise Greenfield. Thank-you, Eloise Greenfield." Children respond favorably to this routine and, after a few times, insist on naming the poet if you forget!
- Read the poem once so children can enjoy the sound of the words and the poem's ideas. Interactive poems, like "Sand" and "My True Story" invite children to join in on the first reading. Since children often follow the model they see and hear during the first reading of a poem, you'll want to read expressively.
- Read and reread each new poem to allow children to think about what they have heard before they join in to repeat inflections or gestures you've modeled.
- You can readily identify a "good" poem when children ask eagerly to hear it again. If responses are not what you expected, try reintroducing the poem at a later time. Perhaps you'll read in a different rhythm, experiment with inflections and gestures, or provide additional introductory discussion.

Dramatizing Poems Children can present impromptu dramatizations or plan and rehearse a production that includes several poems around a theme. Poems such as "Mixed Up Me," "Hiding," "Six Speckled Hens," "Humpty Dumpty," "Copycat," "Dancing," and "Glug! Gurgle! Glug!" lend themselves to dramatization. Use "Chucka-chucka Choo Choo," "El Train," "The Train," "Subway," and "Boxcars" for a program about trains, or focus on safety with "Signs," "Streets," "Yes or No," "Stop, Drop, and Roll," "Stop Sign's Song," "Stop, Look, Listen," "Emergency," "Alas!", "Traffic Light," and "Where's My Seat Belt?"

Enjoying Fingerplays and Action Rhymes
Children develop their small and large motor skills and feel good about themselves when they participate in rhythmic movement activities. The many fingerplays and hand rhymes, such as "Morning Exercises" or "Beehive," exercise the small muscles and are good for quiet times or when space is limited. Numerous action rhymes, such as "Elephant" or "Mixed-up Me," involve whole-body movement and provide outlets for energy during periods of transition.

Writing Poems Try the following ideas to help young children create their own poems.
• Use lists to generate new poem topics. Help children list the kinds of berries in "The Berry Family" or the rhyming words in "Mr. Bear." Encourage them to add to the lists or make new ones and think about how the words might fit together to create original poems.
• Practice oral innovations on familiar texts and then model writing the new words.
• Read "Jack and Jill" and "Alas!," and write more parodies of nursery rhymes. Create new lyrics to familiar tunes.
• Children can "feel" a poem's rhythm by clapping it or reading it as a rap or song. Help children follow the meter to add original lines or say and write new poems.

Celebrating Cultural Diversity Share poems that introduce children to words and rhythms of several languages: "Wild Geese," "Happy Birthday to Me," "Un elefante se balanceaba," "The Train," Grano con grano," "Toy Tik Ka," "My Nipa Hut-Bakay Kubo," and "La rosas tienen."

Opening and Closing Poetry Sessions
Many teachers establish routines for beginning and ending poetry time. Try opening your poetry periods with "I love," "A Friend," or a favorite of your own. Take advantage of the quieting effect of "Fog" or the inner stillness evoked by "Deep in the Forest" before children move on to the next activity.

8

Me

Unit 1

Mud Monster

by BONNIE KINNE

Introducing the Poem
Tell children the title and then read or recite the poem as if you're telling a story that happened to you. Encourage children to share stories about times they've stepped in mud. Then invite children to pantomime the poem as you reread it or play the recording.

Dramatizing the Poem
Invite children to take turns wearing boots over shoes and socks, and say the poem as partners pretend to be mud monsters who pull them off one-by-one.

Talking about Monsters
Help children talk about why the mud seems like a monster as its suction grabs at boots, shoes, and socks. Talk about why monsters can't be real.

Encourage children to tell about monsters they've seen in books or on TV and tell why each is friendly or scary. Invite children to dramatize how each monster acts. Children might substitute other monsters' names in the poem and change other words as needed.

Exploring Size Relationships
Children will enjoy stacking and nesting different sized paper cups, recycled tin cans, and mixing cups and bowls.

Sorting Clothes
Provide two or more pairs of socks, shoes, and boots, if possible, in varying sizes and colors. Invite children to sort the items and match the pairs. Encourage children to ask family members to help them sort pairs of socks at home at laundry time.

Exploring Suction
Have children pretend that nested paper cups are boots, shoes, and socks. Help children say the poem as they press the upright cups into mud and then lift gently to allow the mud to "gobble" the bottom cup. Encourage children to experiment to see if the mud will always gobble the bottom cup.

Molding Mud Shapes
Help children mix soil, water, and dried grass clippings to a thick gooey consistency. Pour the mud into various containers such as foil-lined cupcake tins, candy molds, or paper cups. Children might use recycled milk cartons to make building bricks to use in building structures. Allow the mud to dry thoroughly before removing the mold.

Enjoying Related Literature
Read *Harry and the Terrible Whatzit* by Dick Gackenbach, Maurice Sendak's *Where the Wild Things Are*, *Amy's Monster* by Jenny Wagner, and *Mud Puddle* by Robert N. Munch. Share "The Purple People Eater" (Adventure: Theme Opener).

Activity Page 1: Sorting Muddy Clothes
Reproduce the page for each child. Help children cut out each laundry bag and fold on the dotted line. Have children staple the sides of each bag and then cut out the pictures of soiled clothes and put each in its correct bag.

Activity Page 2: Dressing Feet
Reproduce the page for each child. Help children identify the feet, socks, shoes, and boots that are pointing to the right and left. Have children cut out the pictures and "dress" each pair of feet by placing the appropriate pictures on top of each other. Help children staple each "book" together at the top and then flip the pages as they say the poem.

Mud Monster

The mud monster
Gobbled up my boots.
Then he gobbled up my shoes,
And he started on my socks,
But before he reached my toes,
I yelled Helllllllllp!

Bonnie Kinne

"Mud Monster" by Bonnie Kinne.
Reprinted by permission of the author.

Sorting Muddy Clothes

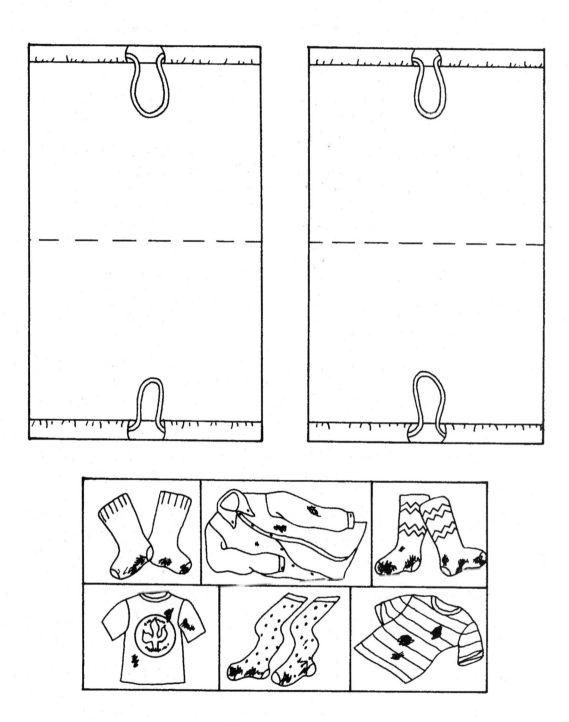

Cut out each laundry bag, fold on the dotted line, and
staple the sides together. Cut out the pictures of soiled
clothes and sort the dirty laundry into the correct bags.

12

Dressing Feet

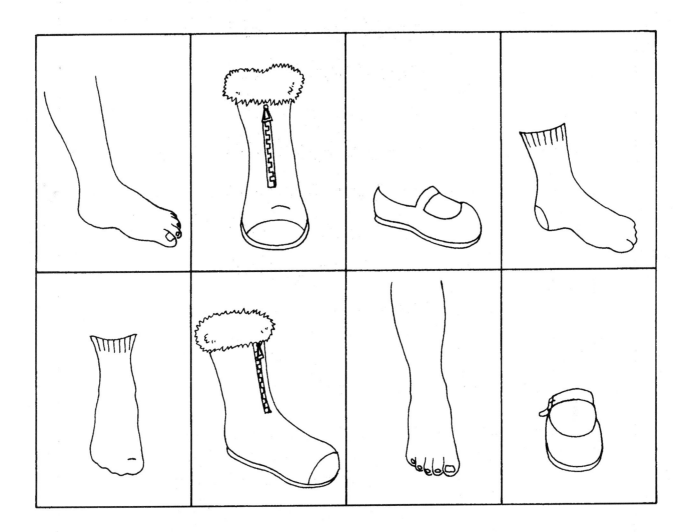

Cut out the pictures. Put socks, shoes, and boots on each foot and staple the pictures together at the top. Flip the pages to show how the Mud Monster tries to get your toes.

I love

by ELOISE GREENFIELD

Living with the Poem's Words

This is a good poem to recite spontaneously whenever you're feeling good and want the world to know it. You may want to add, "Thank you, Eloise Greenfield, for giving me words to say how I feel right now!" Watch children follow your model to share their good feelings about being alive!

Sharing the Words in Print

Display the poster and encourage children to recite with you as you track familiar words. Talk about what the child in the illustration is doing and why.

Compare the lengths of words such as *I* and *yesterday* or *you* and *although*, help children find the word *day* in *today* and *yesterday,* or count the times the poet used the words *you* or *I.*

Showing Love

Encourage children to tell about ways they show love to themselves, other people, animals, places, and things. In addition to giving hugs, kisses, and gifts, include ideas such as cleaning and feeding our bodies, sharing, spending time together, brushing teeth, feeding pets, saying kind things, revisiting favorite places, taking care of books, and putting toys away.

Innovating on the Text

Talk about the sweet taste of honey and the word's use as a sweet and special name for a loved one. Children can share special names their families use and place sticky tabs on the poster to substitute their words for *honey.*

Using a Symbol for Love

Say each word as you write "I love cats" on chart paper. (This is a good time to mention that you've used a period to show where your sentence ends.)

Track the words as you reread the sentence. Then say each word as you write "I ❤ cats" under the first sentence. Ask what word the heart symbol stands for. Have children tell about things they love as you write their words in sentences such as *Winona says, "I ❤ peaches."* Invite children to read their words. Cut sentences into strips for children to glue on drawing paper and illustrate. Children can share their words with family members at home.

To publish heart-shaped "I Love" books, invite each child to dictate several sentence strips. Encourage using the poet's model to end with "I love ME, too!" Book covers might include Eloise Greenfield's poem.

Charting People, Places, and Things

Title a large chart or bulletin board "We Love!" Have children help list their names down the left side and these headings above three wide columns: *People, Places, Things.* Invite each child to draw or cut out and glue pictures of one person, one place, and one thing he or she loves. You may want to allow room for children's photos beside their names or add a column titled *Animals.*

Making "I Love" Collages

Provide red paper hearts or have children paint cardboard hearts red. Invite children to cut out pictures of things they love and glue them on the hearts.

Share Miriam Cohen's *Bee My Valentine,* Margery Cuyler's *Freckles and Willie: A Valentine's Day Story*, or *Arthur's Great Big Valentine* by Lillian Hoban.

Enjoying More Literature

Read about Michelle Edwards' *Chicken Man* who loves many things, including himself. Introduce or review "Grandpa" (Home and Family: Poster 8),"Toy Tik Ka," "A Fall of Colors," "You," "Keziah," "Lucky," "Valentine Feelings," and Eloise Greenfield's "By Myself" (all in Related Read-Alouds). Share more of the poet's work in her collection titled *Honey, I love and other love poems.*

I love

I love

I love a lot of things

A whole lot of things

And honey,

I love ME, too

Eloise Greenfield

"I love" from HONEY, I LOVE by Eloise Greenfield. Text copyright © 1978 by Eloise Greenfield. Selection reprinted by permission of HarperCollins Publishers.

All About Me

by DONNA LUGG PAPE

Telling a Picture's Story

To help children recognize that a picture tells a story, display a photo or picture from a magazine. Tell children the picture tells a story, but the story hasn't been written in words yet. Ask who the characters would be, where the story takes place, and what is happening. Help children put their words into three or four sentences you write on chart paper. Reread the story.

Provide experiences in telling and writing more stories about the same picture. Repeat this activity over several days before introducing the printless poster and the poem.

Introducing the Poem

Display the printless poster and encourage thought about whether the adult might be a grandmother, aunt, or other relative, why the woman is making the wall hanging, and whose pictures are on the quilt. Have children predict how the photo that will be placed in the quilt's blank square will look. Invite children to dictate their story.

Display a transparency of the poem and tell children that the poster's story might also be told in a poem. Read the title and ask who in the illustration might say the words. Invite children to listen to more words the child might say. On the second reading, children can pretend to be the child in the picture and dramatize the feelings.

Enjoying Rhyme

Dramatize crying, being sleepy, peeping from behind something, and sweeping with a broom as you say, "I'm a weepy me, a sleepy me, a peepy me, a sweepy me." Encourage children to add other real or coined "eepy" words. Repeat for *wiggly/giggly* or *scary/merry*.

Building Vocabulary

Help children realize that while facial features alone can show a "weepy me," it takes the whole body to show a "wiggly me." Ask how people act when they feel weepy (cry, weep, sob), sleepy (yawn, rub eyes, go to bed), or giggly (laugh, chuckle).

Help children extend the poem with word pairs such as *hungry/gobbly, hot/sweaty,* or *crooked/wobbly.*

Capturing Expressions

Enlist the help of volunteers to take snapshots of each child's different expressions. Mount photos singly or collectively and invite children to dictate captions such as "I'm a happy me." Bind as personal photo albums to be shared at home, display on a bulletin board titled "All About Me," or create a photograph quilt as depicted on the poster.

Feeling One Way or Another

To help children talk about how and why feelings change, tell and dramatize several sentences that suggest cause and effect. Examples might be "I felt giggly until I heard a strange noise, and then I felt scared" or "I felt weepy until Dad came, and then I felt happy." You may want to pause for children to supply the second emotion. Children might illustrate sentences they initiate.

Creating Expressions

Provide materials such as buttons, marbles, nuts in shells, and drinking straws cut to varying lengths. At the sand table, invite children to use them to create faces with different expressions. When finished, children can sift the sand and sort the materials for reuse.

Children might glue similar materials on paper plates or craft paper bag puppets named "Sleepy," "Weepy," or "Scary."

Enjoying Related Literature

Share *Feelings* by Aliki, Grimms' *Snow White* retold by Nancy Garden or Randall Jarrell's picture book translation of the story, and Related Read-Alouds, "My Faces," "Valentine Feelings," "I Look Pretty," "Everybody Says," "Freckles," "This Tooth," "Brownish-Sandy Cotton Candy," "If Only I Could Fly," "A bright red poppy," and "Look at Me!"

All About Me

Whenever I'm sad,
I'm a weepy me.
Whenever I'm tired,
I'm a sleepy me.
If I can't sit still,
I'm a wiggly me.
When I'm full of laughs,
I'm a giggly me.
If I shout BOO!
I'm a scary me.
If I feel happy,
I'm a merry me.
Weepy
    Sleepy
        Wiggly
            Giggly
                Scary
                    Merry

    ME!

Donna Lugg Pape

"All About Me" by Donna Lugg Pape.
Reprinted by permission of the author.

Mixed-Up Me

by WILMA YEO

Previewing Vocabulary
Invite children to exercise with you to preview some of the words and ideas from the poem. Children might chant "head, feet, waist" or "up, down, middle" as they stretch.

Introducing the Poem
You may want to introduce this poem in the gym or around a floor mat. Display the poster and read the poem's title. Ask which child in the illustration might say the words and why. Read the poem aloud and then encourage children to say the words with you as they dramatize the poem. Invite children to demonstrate somersaults or other movements where the body appears to be mixed up. Help children notice that their waists are always in the middle. Allow time for repeated readings that not only provide fun and exercise, but also help children learn the poem.

Identifying Up, Down, and Middle
Talk about other body parts that are up, down, and in the middle. Then challenge children to complete ideas such as "My head is up. My hips are down. My chest is (in the middle)" or "My knees are up. My toes are down. My ankles are (in the middle)." Variations could include children in the middle between ceiling and floor, a tree's trunk in the middle between its branches and roots, or a person in the middle of a group.

Speaking as Observers
Using a doll or stuffed animal, model dramatizing the poem as if the toy is speaking. Then pretend to speak *to* the character as you change the words *I* and *my* to *your* and *you*. Help some children be observers who say the poem as others act it out.

Creating Mixed-Up Characters
Reproduce and enlarge the three animal pictures for each child. (See page 271.) Allow time for coloring, if desired. Then assist children in drawing guide lines and cutting on the lines to divide each picture into thirds. Encourage children to experiment by mixing up the animals' tops, middles, and bottoms to create mixed up characters.

Learning about an Unusual Animal
Share John Hoke's *Discovering the World of the Three-toed Sloth* or show children a picture of a sloth, a South American animal. Talk about how the sloth hangs upside down from tree limbs and even eats, sleeps, and moves along the limbs in that "mixed up" position. Point out that humans might also think of the sloth as being mixed up since it sleeps during the day! Help children locate South America on a map.

Making Mixed Up Treats
Invite children to use sandwich fillings and different kinds of crackers, breads, or vegetable slices to make mixed up sandwiches whose tops and bottoms are different. Children might also help prepare a layered gelatin or an upside-down cake.

Enjoying Related Literature
Two poems from the Related Read-Alouds illustrate mixed up ideas. Share "Eletelephony" and discuss how the poet has mixed up two words. Reread the poem, this time modeling an "Uh-oh" gesture such as clapping your hand to your mouth after saying each mixed-up word. Encourage children to join you in "catching" each mixed-up word. Ask children to listen for two ways the clown is mixed up in the poem "Inside Outside Upside Down."

Children will enjoy the humorous mixed-up situations in Peggy Parish's *Amelia Bedelia* books and in the *Morris and Boris* books by Bernard Wiseman.

Mixed-Up Me

My head is up
My feet are down
My waist is in the middle
But when I turn a somersault,
I mix them up a little!

Wilma Yeo

"Mix-Up Me" by Wilma Yeo.
Used by permission of the author.

RESPONDING To

My Bones

by BABS BELL HAJDUSIEWICZ

Introducing the Poem
To stimulate interest in the first reading, omit the title and read or recite the poem in a conversational tone, as if you're telling a story about yourself. Encourage children to stretch with you to touch each body part named. Try reading the poem faster, or have volunteers demonstrate the actions.

Singing the Poem's Words
Sing the poem's words to warm up at exercise time or simply to stretch those wiggles away.

Identifying Body Parts
Help children identify other body parts where bones hide. Children might add stanzas for *hands, ribs, elbows, shins,* or *thighs* and then dramatize the new verses.

Learning about the Skeleton
Talk about the setting in the illustration. Share *The Skeleton Inside You* by Philip Balestrino or *Outside and Inside You* by Sandra Markle. Have children identify pictured body parts as others recite the poem or sing the song.

Invite a medical professional to share a skeleton model and X-ray pictures and possibly introduce children to other technology, such as the CAT Scan or sonogram, that allows physicians to see inside the body.

Playing "Boney-Pokey"
Play "Hokey-Pokey" as a circle game. Then help children substitute *arm bones, leg bones,* and so on to do the "Boney-Pokey."

Learning about the Funny Bone
Ask children where they think a funny bone hides. Explain that "funny bone" and "crazy bone" are names for the bone at the elbow. Help children notice that the elbow bone has little protection in comparison to bones in the thighs or arms. Tell about a time you bumped your elbow and how the painful feeling was more peculiar or odd than laughable.

Hiding "Bones"
Read "Skeleton's Clothes" (Related Read-Alouds) and talk about how muscles cover bones and skin covers muscles. Provide materials such as popsicle sticks, clay, and cheesecloth or tissue paper. Help children decide which materials might best represent bones, muscles, or skin. Reread "Skeleton's Clothes" as children work to hide "bones." Sing "My Bones" as children try to feel the "bones."

Mending Broken "Bones"
Talk about how broken bones heal when the pieces are held immobile while calcium builds up around the break. Provide tape and broken twigs or popsicle sticks. Invite children to bandage the broken "bones" or set them in clay casts. A visit from a medical professional would be ideal for this activity. Introduce "Skerbonker Doodles" (Related Read-Alouds).

Making Models of Finger Bones
Children will enjoy watching you model this activity before they participate. Draw around your hand on a piece of paper. Then bend your index finger and count the three short bones. Count out three pieces of popsicle stick or other material to represent the bones and glue them onto the index finger on paper. Continue for your other fingers, and then help children make similar models of their finger bones on paper or old gloves. Suggest that children repeat the activity for a family member's fingers.

This is a good time to introduce "Hinges" (Related Read-Alouds) and explore how joints such as elbows or knees act like hinges on a door.

Making Size Comparisons
Discuss how bones grow as we grow bigger. Read "I Am Growing!" (Related Read-Alouds) and have children play-act growing bigger and bigger.

See Adding Music, page 176.
See Meet the Poet, page 189.

My Bones

My skeleton tries its best to hide
But I can feel my bones inside
My arms
My legs
My shoulders
My toes
My ankles
My fingers
My knees
My nose
My skeleton tries its best to hide
But I can feel my bones inside!

Babs Bell Hajdusiewicz

Happy Birthday to Me!

by CARMEN MUÑOZ

Setting the Stage

Ask what the children in the poster's illustration are celebrating. Model using the words *dulces* and *candy* or *¡Feliz Cumpleaños!* and *Happy Birthday* interchangeably as children use the illustration to support their ideas. Invite children who've had experience with piñatas to describe the shapes and colors of the piñatas and tell about finding candy and other goodies inside.

Introducing the Poem

Read the title and ask which child in the illustration might be saying the words. Have children listen as you read and track more words the birthday child says. Tell children the poet wrote this poem in English but used some Spanish words, too. Reread the poem and point out how the words *¡Feliz Cumpleaños!* and *Happy Birthday!* compare in appearance and sound.

At another time, explore Charlotte Pomerantz's use of Vietnamese words in "Toy Tik Ka" (Related Read-Alouds) or share books such as Rebecca Emberley's *Taking a Walk/Caminado: A Book in Two Languages* or *Uncle Nacho's Hat/El Sombrero del tio Nacho* by Harriet Rohmer.

Using a Map or Globe

Talk about how Spanish is one of many languages spoken by people in the United States. Help children place sticky tabs on a map to locate other countries such as Mexico, Spain, or Central and South American countries where Spanish is spoken. You may also want to locate countries where other languages are spoken.

Making Piñatas

Make a paper maché piñata by applying layers of pasted newspaper strips over an inflated balloon. Paint or decorate the dried form, cut an opening, and fill with treats. Children can make individual piñatas with squares of tissue paper and twist ties.

Singing Birthday Greetings

Invite children to sing "Happy Birthday" to the child in the illustration. Then have children pretend to be the birthday child and sing "Happy Birthday to Me!" to the same tune. Encourage children to share birthday songs they know in other languages.

Sharing Birthday Traditions

Talk about how family and friends, a piñata, a birthday cake and candles, or a party are part of many people's birthday celebrations. Tell children about any special activities, gifts, or foods that are part of birthday celebrations in your family. Children will enjoy playing the roles of your family members or using puppets to act out a birthday celebration in your home. Then encourage children to share birthday traditions their families enjoy.

Celebrating Birthdays

Establish a classroom tradition for children's birthdays by sharing the poster and inviting the celebrant to read and sing the poem's words with you. You might also read *Happy Birthday, Moon* by Frank Asch or Anne and Harlow Rockwell's *Happy Birthday to Me.* Other selections for honoring a birthday child, celebrating famous people's birthdays, or having an "unbirthday" party might be "Birthday Wish," "Birthday Piñata," or "A Special Day" (all in Related Read-Alouds) or Tom Chapin's recording "Happy Birthday."

Making a Birthday Tree

At the beginning of the school year, have children help draw a large tree for a bulletin board or set a bare branch in a pot. Mount children's photos on colored paper circles and help children write their names and birthdates. Designate a spot for each month and have children attach their photos.

See Meet the Poets, Page191.

Happy Birthday to Me!

My piñata is hanging
from my favorite tree.
Are there *dulces* and cookies
for friends and for me?

I'm happy, as happy,
as happy can be!
¡Feliz Cumpleaños!
Happy   Birthday   to me!

Carmen Muñoz

"Happy Birthday to Me!" by Carmen Muñoz.
Used by permission of the author.

from Fighting Makes No Sense!

by BABS BELL HAJDUSIEWICZ

Building on Prior Knowledge

Before displaying the poster, have children identify their ears, eyes, nose, tongue, and fingers and tell what each does. Then ask children to name or point to body parts to solve riddles such as "I am for smelling. What am I?" Encourage children to share the riddles at home.

Making Sense and Nonsense

Say, "We hear with our noses. No, that doesn't make sense! We hear with our ears!" Repeat more misstatements about the senses and invite children to join in to correct each. Then add sentences such as "We taste with our tongues and that makes sense! We **do** taste with our tongues!" Invite children to initiate sentences for classmates to tell which make sense or are *nonsense*.

Introducing the Poem

Read the title and ask children to listen to the poem to find out who had a fight. Discuss why each body part might think it was best.

Dramatizing the Poem

Point out the word *from* in the poem's title and remind children that the poet wrote more about the body parts' fight. Ask children to think about the meaning of *bragged* as they listen to the recorded poem or to your dramatization of the characters' words. Children will enjoy performing the poem for friends or family members.

Enjoying Rhyme

Have children listen for the word that ends with the same sound as *fight* as you read the first stanza. List more words that rhyme. Repeat for *best* and *rest*.

Learning How Senses Cooperate

Provide items such as crayons, toys, or foods. Children can use one sense to identify an item and another sense to tell more, such as its color, its texture, what it's used for, or who owns it.

Matching One to One

Provide body parts patterns and blank paper . Help each child draw around the spread fingers of one hand, count five fingers and body parts, and cut out and glue one picture on each finger of the paper hand. Invite children to say with you, "I have five senses. My ears hear. My eyes see. My nose smells. My tongue tastes. My fingers feel."

Singing about the Senses

Using the tune "Hot Cross Buns" (see Adding Music), sing "I can smell. I can smell. Flowers, popcorn, pancakes cooking– I can smell." Then substitute the names of other things children can smell. Repeat for the other senses. For variations, include items that are red, begin with the same sound, or are found in the same room at home.

Help children publish the words they've sung. For each book, you'll need three pages with the "I can..." caption and two or three blank pages. Children can draw pictures of themselves using the sense on each captioned page and glue pictures of items on the blank pages.

Share Aliki's *My Five Senses* or sing "My Five Senses" (Related Read-Alouds) to the tune of "Old MacDonald Had a Farm."

Enjoying Related Literature

Share *I Touch* by Rachel Isadora, *Tasting* by Henry Pluckrose, *First Delights: A Book about the Five Senses* by Tasha Tudor, *Touch Will Tell* by Marcia Wise, or the newly revised *Listening Walk* by Paul Showers.

Read "Thumb Says" (Related Read-Alouds) and discuss why a thumb might say, "Fighting makes no sense!" Share "Sounds," "Ears Hear," "Gramps and I," and "I Left My Head" (all in Related Read-Alouds).

See Meet the Poets, page 189.

Fighting Makes No Sense!

My ears
And eyes
And nose
And tongue
And fingers had a fight.
Each part of me
Said it was best
And each thought it was right.

"Sounds to hear are everywhere!"
My ears bragged to the rest.
"None of you can hear those sounds,
So that makes Ears the best!"

"Sights to see are everywhere!"
My eyes bragged to the rest.
"None of you can see those sights,
So that makes Eyes the best!"

"Smells to sniff are everywhere!"
My nose bragged to the rest.
"None of you can sniff those smells,
So that makes Nose the best!"

"Tastes to taste are everywhere!"
My tongue bragged to the rest.
"None of you can taste those tastes,
So that makes Tongue the best!"

"Things to touch are everywhere!"
My hands bragged to the rest.
"Our fingers touch and feel those things,
So that makes Fingers best!"

Then I said, "Fighting makes no sense!
All five of you are best!
Not one can do the other's job,
But...each sense helps the rest."

Babs Bell Hajdusiewicz

I Like You

by MASUHITO

Setting the Stage

Prior to introducing the poem, make a point of commenting to your image in a mirror. You might say, "Hi there! I like you!" or "Goodness, you look like me!" or even tell yourself to cheer up with "Come on, you! Smile!"

Introducing the Poem

Display the poster and read the poem's title. Ask who's saying the words and to whom. Then ask children to listen as you play the recording or read the short poem the child says to herself in the mirror.

Reread the poem to a child and then tell the child some things you like about him or her. Help partners repeat the poem and encourage them tell things they like about each other.

Seeing Reflections

Encourage children to chant the poem with you as they explore their reflections in mirrors of various sizes and kinds, in metal spoons, shiny pans, aluminum foil, window panes, or other surfaces that reflect light. Encourage children to point to themselves for each "you."

Provide aluminum foil and plastic or foam plates for children to make personal mirrors. Children might tape the poem to their mirrors to share at home with family members.

Use mirrors to dramatize other poems such as "All About Me" (Me: Poster 2), "My Faces," "Looking Glass," "Special Me," or "Look at Me!" (all in Related Read-Alouds).

Saying "I Like You!"

Provide old greeting cards or colored paper and reduced copies of the poem for children to create greeting cards for family members, friends, pets, or even cherished toys.

Jumping Through Time

You may want to take children into a gym or outdoors for this activity. Provide a strip of butcher-type paper approximately 24" long for each child. Help children use yardsticks to section the strips into four rectangles approximately 8" x 24" each. Help children paint their first rectangles yellow to suggest *tomorrow*, draw around their feet on their second blocks to suggest the present, or *today,* and paint other colors or symbols on the third and fourth blocks to represent *yesterday* and *the day before yesterday*, respectively. Invite children to stand on the *today* block and jump forward to *tomorrow* or backward to *yesterday* and backward again to *the day before yesterday*. Then have children begin on *the day before yesterday* and "jump through time" as you read the poem.

Using a Calendar

Using a large calendar of the current month, help children identify *today, tomorrow, yesterday,* and *the day before yesterday.* Invite a volunteer to point to *the day before yesterday* and do "finger jumps" to illustrate the poem's words as you read.

Living with the Poem's Words

Recite the poem on a Wednesday and again the next day as children leave to go home. On Friday, use a sticky tab on the poster to change *tomorrow* to *Monday*. Then help children consult the calendar on Monday and again on Tuesday to innovate on the text or omit words as appropriate. You may want to create a poster for each day's version of the poem or play a recording of "Tomorrow" from the musical *Annie.*

At other times model substituting *this morning* for *the day before yesterday* and *this afternoon* for *yesterday and today*.

Learning about the Poet

Tell children the poet lived more than one thousand years ago or nearly half a million yesterdays ago in the part of the world that is now Japan. Help children locate Japan on a map or globe.

I Like You

Although I saw you

The day before yesterday,

And yesterday and today,

This much is true—

I want to see you tomorrow, too!

Masuhito

"I Like You" reprinted with permission of Charles Scribner's Sons,
an imprint of Macmillan Publishing Company,
from I LIKE YOU AND OTHER POEMS OF VALENTINE'S DAY.

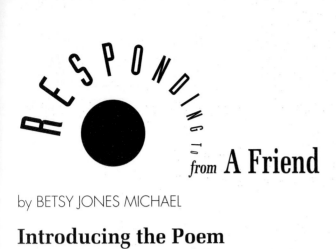

from **A Friend**

by BETSY JONES MICHAEL

Introducing the Poem

Invite discussion about the illustration before reading the poem's title. Then help children use the illustration and title to predict what the poem might be about. Read the poem and talk about how it feels and why it's fun to have a friend.

Seeing How Print Works

Track the poem's words as you read and encourage children to think about why the poet used capital letters for *HURRAY*. Reread, and pause for children to join in on *HURRAY*.

Rewrite the poem's fourth line to substitute words like *YIPPEE* or *WHOOPIE* for *HURRAY*. Then substitute *whisper* for *shout* and write *shhhh* in tiny letters.

Enjoying More of the Poet's Words

Point out the word *from* in the poem's title and explain that the poet wrote more about the fun of having a friend. Read the complete poem for children to name more ways friends have fun together. You may want to share a transparency of the whole poem.

Dramatizing the Poem

Ask when friends "might not even talk" or what friends might giggle about or learn together. Then help partners act out the poem as you read aloud.

Model using the poet's words whenever you observe children working and playing together.

Singing the Poem

Review the idea that when we add music to a poem, we create a song. Invite children to dramatize the poem as they sing along with the recording.

Discussing Friendship

Initiate discussion about friendship by telling children the name of a friend of yours and something you like about him or her. Encourage children to follow your model to tell things they like about their friends.

Discuss and have children act out some ways friends help each other. Examples might be sharing a book, cooperating to lift a box of toys, or showing concern when someone is hurt or sad. This is a good time to introduce or review "I'm Sharing" (Community: Poster 7).

Sharing Friends with Friends

Help each child draw around an oval-shaped pattern and glue on materials such as macaroni, colored paper scraps, and yarn to share a special friend's face. Write each child's words that tell the friend's name and what the child likes to do with that friend. Help children write their own names and then display all the special friends under the caption *It's Fun to Have a Friend!*

Building Vocabulary

Using sticky tabs, show children how other words such as *pal, buddy,* or *chum* might be substituted in the poem for *friend,* and *good, great,* or *nice* might be substituted for *fun.*

Enjoying More Poems about Friends

Share "two friends" (Community: Poster 4), "My Friends" (Community: Poster 6), or "Grandpa" (Home and Family: Poster 8). Help children think about other kinds of friendships as suggested in "I Like You" (Me: Poster 7), "Hey, Bug!" (Nature: Theme Opener), "Sun Fun," or "Thumb Says" (both in Related Read-Alouds).

Reading Related Literature

Read about friendship in James Marshall's *George and Martha,* Arnold Lobel's *Frog and Toad* books, *Will I Have a Friend?* and *Best Friends* by Miriam Cohen, *We are Best Friends* by Aliki, or Eric Carle's *Do You Want to Be My Friend?* Difficulties in friendships are addressed in *Best Friends for Frances* by Russell Hoban, *I'm Not Oscar's Friend Any More* by Marjorie Sharmat, and in Holly Keller's *Lizzie's Invitation.*

See Adding Music, page 169.

A Friend

It's fun to have a friend!
Someone to see and stay with
To walk and talk and play with
To laugh and shout HURRAY with
It's fun to have a friend!

We might not even talk!
We might just sit and giggle
Until we wiggle-wiggle
Or leap and jump and jiggle
We might not even talk!

It's fun to have a friend!
To hold a hand and go with
To ask and learn and know with
To sing and dance and grow with
It's fun to have a friend!

Betsy Jones Michael

"A Friend" by Betsy Jones Michael.
Reprinted by permission of the author.

RESPONDING To

I Can!

by BABS BELL HAJDUSIEWICZ

Introducing the Poem
Display the poster and read the poem aloud. Ask what the child is doing in each illustration. Invite children to dramatize as you reread the poem or play the recording.

Giving Meaning to Print
Track the words as you read the poem. Reread each sentence and help the children identify its illustration.

Learning about Tools
Talk about when and why we use tools such as a broom, a mop, or a saw. Emphasize how each of these hand tools needs our energy to make it work. Help children name more hand tools such as sponges, hammers, or toothbrushes that are used for cleaning or building. Invite children to dramatize using their energy to make each tool work.

Discuss how tools such as vacuums or power saws get energy to work from motors powered by batteries or electricity. If possible, provide experience with hand and power versions of tools such as a juicer or pencil sharpener. Share "Our Washing Machine" (Home and Family: Poster 2) and "Vacuum" and "Toaster Time" (Related Read-Alouds). Encourage children to look for uses of hand and power tools at home.

Exploring Ways to be Helpful
Discuss how we help ourselves and others when we can clean a sink or sweep a floor. Ask children who they help when they fold laundry, sort trash for recycling, or spend time with someone who is ill or lonely. As opportunities arise, help children be aware of things they can do that are helpful to themselves and others.

You may want to introduce "Yes or No" (Related Read-Alouds) and discuss how we help ourselves when we make decisions about what we will or won't do.

Feeling the Rhythm
Encourage children to join in to clap or tap a rhythm to accompany the poem (ta-ta-ta/ta-ta-ta/ta-ta-ta-ta-ta-ta-ta). Vary the activity by substituting *we* or children's names for *I*, or model how other words, such as *Work and play/Work and play/Look what I can do today* can be chanted to the same rhythm.

Telling and Asking
To model the use of complete sentences when speaking, dramatize the action as you say, "I can brush my hair. What can you do?" Help children follow your model to tell what they can do and then ask what peers can do.

Repeat for wishes such as "I wish I could _____. What do you wish you could do?"

Share a picture of Auguste Rodin's sculpture *The Thinker.* Children can strike a similar pose and tell what they can think about.

Viewing Talk Written Down
Repeat children's words about what they can do as you write sentences such as *Sudra says, "I can feed my cat"* or *Arnie says, "I can dress myself"* in list form on chart paper. Read the sentences and pause for children to read their own words.

Attach each child's sentence strip to a sheet of drawing paper. Children will enjoy illustrating their words and then sharing what they have said with family members at home.

Children might recall and illustrate what others have said about them, such as "My grandma likes how I can stir the cookie dough" or "My dad says I can make him laugh."

Enjoying Related Books
Share Shlego Watanabe's humorous books, *I Can Ride It, I Can Build a House,* and *I Can Take a Walk,* or any of Peggy Parish's books in the *See and Do* series.

See Meet the Poets, page 189.

I Can!

I can count.
I can hop.
I can use a broom and mop.
I can dance.
I can draw.
I can build things with a saw.
I can wink.
I can think.
I can clean the bathroom sink.
I can read.
I can sing.
I can do most anything!

Babs Bell Hajdusiewicz

"I Can" © 1990 by Babs Bell Hajdusiewicz.
Reprinted by permission of the author.

Home and Family

Unit 2

Goops (Table Manners)

by GELETT BURGESS

Introducing the Poem
Children will love watching you act the part of a Goop as you pretend to lick your fingers and a knife, act like you're tipping a bowl, make exaggerated chewing motions, and show an expression of extreme dislike while placing your hands on your hips. Although children will be eager to say they're not Goops, they'll be just as eager to act out the Goops' behavior as you reread the poem!

Making and Straining "Soup"
Help children use water and materials such as raw rice, noodles, or pebbles to make "soup." Ask children to describe their soup and tell how they made it. Then provide serrated spoons or a strainer for children to remove all but the "broth."

Describing What Goops Do
Have children name the Goops' disgusting behaviors and more disgusting things they might do, such as sneezing or coughing without covering their mouths, slurping liquids, or grabbing things from others. Introduce or review "I'm Sharing" (Community: Poster 7) and "Sneezing" (Related Read-Alouds).

Talk about how babies eat like Goops until they get bigger and learn manners.

Dramatizing Opposites
Invite children to help set a table for a snack. Then have children take turns being Goops and instructors who show the opposite of each behavior. Encourage children to show family members at home how Goops would and should act.

Exploring a Tongue's Job
Use a tongue depressor to demonstrate why you wouldn't lick a knife like a Goop does. Hold your tongue down while saying, "I can't talk without my tongue." Help children use tongue depressors to experiment similarly.

Talk about how the tongue does another important job, tasting. Invite children to wear blindfolds as they taste foods to identify which are sweet or sour.

Exploring Ways to Chew
Help children name crunchy foods, such as raw vegetables, that can be difficult to eat without making noise. Invite children to observe as you exaggerate the action of biting off a piece of raw carrot and then chew noisily with your mouth open. Encourage children to use the word *disgusting* to describe how it feels to hear and see someone chew food like a Goop. Encourage them to tell how you might make less noise as you bite into and chew a carrot. Then provide carrots for children to chew, first as Goops might and then less noisily.

Enjoying Related Literature
Read more of the poet's work in *Goops and How to Be Them* and *More Goops*. Share *Rotten Ralph* by Jack Gantos, *Gregory, the Terrible Eater* by Mitchell Sharmat, and *What Do You Say, Dear?/What Do You Do, Dear?* by Sesyle Joslin.

Activity Page 3: The Goops Book
Reproduce the page for each child. Have children cut out the title page and pictures and place them in order to tell the story of the Goops. Children might dictate sentences to tell each picture's story and then staple their books.

Activity Page 4: The Goopy Goops
Reproduce the page for each child. Help children cut out the circle and arrow and use a brad to make a spinner. Children can take turns spinning to choose "goopy" behaviors to act out as partners act out the opposite behaviors.

Goops (Table Manners)

The Goops they lick their fingers,
    And the goops they lick their knives;
They spill their broth on the tablecloth—
    Oh, they lead disgusting lives!
The Goops they talk while eating,
    And loud and fast they chew;
And that is why I'm glad that I
    Am not a Goop — are you?

Gelett Burgess

"Goops" by Gelett Burgess.

Activity Page 3: Goops

The Goops' Story

Cut out the pages and arrange them in the correct order to make a book that tells the Goop's story.

The Goopy Goops

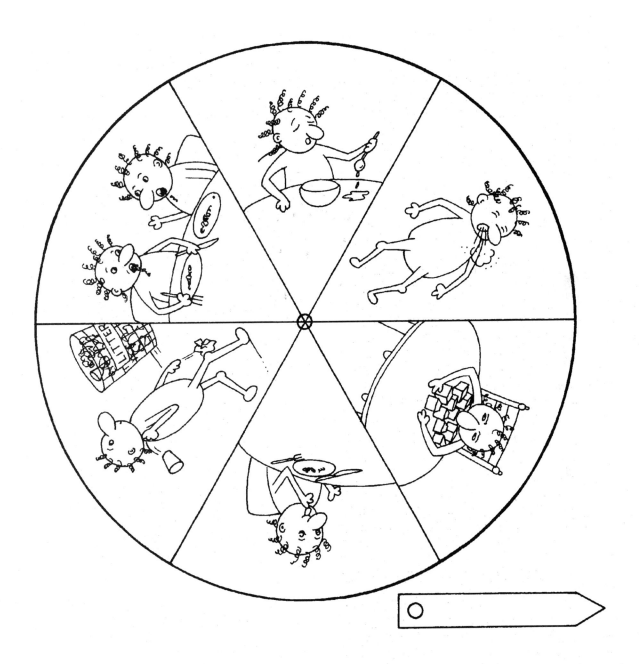

Spin the spinner and act out the Goopy behavior the arrow points to. Then show how the Goops should have acted.

37

from A House Is a House for Me

by MARY ANN HOBERMAN

Assessing Prior Knowledge
Play a riddle game to check children's familiarity with the animals and insects they'll hear about in the poem. Include the animal's sound, its home, or habits in riddles such as, "Bzzzz! I live in a hive and make honey. Who am I?" or "I am a very tiny insect. My name rhymes with *can't*. Who am I?" Help children practice riddles to quiz family members at home.

Introducing the Poem
Invite discussion about the animals and homes in the poster's illustration. On the first reading, try pausing for children to help supply the ending words of lines.

Learning about Animals' Homes
Read Mary Ann Hoberman's complete poem in her book by the same title and share other poems about animals and their homes in "Squirmy Earthworm" (Nature: Poster 7), "Beehive" and "Polka-Dot Caterpillar" (Animals: Posters 4 and 7), or "Turtles," "Bunny," "Old Snake Has Gone to Sleep," "Snail," "Baby Chick," and sing "Tower of Blocks" (all in Related Read-Alouds). Share Leo Lionni's snail story, *The Biggest House in the World*. Invite children to draw or cut out pictures of animals and their homes for a display titled "A House Is a House for Me."

Children can observe ants at work around a lure such as a piece of hard candy. If possible, collect ants and soil in a jar to observe ants building an anthill.

Thinking about More Homes
Stimulate thought about other "homes" in the classroom with sentences such as "The shelf is a home for blocks," "The closet is a home for coats," or "My body is a home for me." Suggest that children look around at home and tell family members where things like toothbrushes, books, a toaster, bicycles, or cereals "live."

Building Homes
Read "The Funny House," "Yesterday's Paper," "Keziah," "Sleeping Outdoors," and "My Nipa Hut" (all in Related Read-Alouds). Provide blocks and other building materials such as twigs, rugs and blankets, rocks and pebbles, and milk cartons for children to build homes and then use the poem's model to tell about them.

Asking Questions to Learn
Encourage children to ask at home about other places they or family members have lived or who family members lived with and where they lived when they were children.

Playing with Rhyme
Reread the poem for children to identify the words that rhyme with *me* (bee, tree), *hole* (mole), *snug* (bug, rug), and *house* (mouse). Allow for "coined" words as children name more words that rhyme with each group.

At other times, help children complete two-line poems that begin with "A house is a house for me" with lines such as "But I would need a key!" or "I couldn't live in the sea." Or challenge children to provide an ending word that rhymes with the first word in sentences such as "*Glass* is a home for *grass*" or "*Ants* are on my *pants*."

Playing with Two-Word Rhymes
Model some "hink-pink" rhymes such as *wee bee, mole hole,* or *snug bug* and help children think of others such as *wee flea, whole bowl,* or *door store.* Try some two-syllable "hinky-pinky" rhymes such as *slinky winky, swishy fishy,* or *letter getter.*

Listening for Beginning Sounds
Have children listen for the sound of *h* in *hill, house, hive,* and *hole* as you reread to accent the sound in the poem's first stanza. Invite children to say the words with you and then name more words that begin with the sound. Repeat for beginning sounds of *m* as in *mole* and *mouse* or *b* as in *bird* and *builds.*

38

from A House Is a House for Me

A hill is a house for an ant, an ant.

A hive is a house for a bee.

A hole is a house for a mole or a mouse,

And a house is a house for me!

A web is a house for a spider.

A bird builds its nest in a tree.

There is nothing so snug as a bug in a rug

And a house is a house for me!

Mary Ann Hoberman

"A House Is a House For Me" reprinted by
permission of Gina Maccoby Literary Agency.
Copyright © 1978 by Mary Ann Hoberman.

Our Washing Machine

by PATRICIA HUBBELL

Setting the Stage
Invite children to join in as you dramatize washing clothes while singing "The Mulberry Bush." Ask why we wash our clothes, and then invite children to dramatize and sing their words to the same tune for verses such as "We wash our clothes to make them clean..." or "We wash our clothes 'cause they are dirty...." Children might innovate similarly for other verses from the song.

Introducing the Poem
Display the poster and read the poem's title. If necessary, help children recognize that the washing machine in the illustration has broken. Invite children to imitate sounds they might expect to hear in a poem about a broken washer. For repeated readings, children might listen for a word that tells the time shown on the clock in the picture, or groups might say the washer's sounds chorally.

Learning about Energy
Talk about how some people use their own energy to wash clothes on washboards or on rocks and then hang the clothes outside for the wind's energy to dry them. Model use of the word *automatic* to discuss how a washer or dryer gets energy from electricity to do the same work. Help children name more kinds of machines and tell which use electricity. How do families clean dishes, dry hair, cook and chill food, or heat and cool their homes? Share "Toaster Time," "Vacuum" (both in Related Read-Alouds), and poems in Jill Bennett's collection, *Machine Poems*.

Cleaning Dirty Clothes
Provide washboards, tubs, soap powder, some slightly soiled washcloths or other cloth pieces, a clothesline, and clothespins. Model innovating on "The Mulberry Bush" for each step as children scrub, rinse, and then hang up their laundry to dry.

Making a Washing Machine
Share "Swish, swash" (Related Read-Alouds). Then invite children to make a "Swish, Swash" washing machine using a clear plastic container with a tight-fitting lid. Place a soiled cloth in the "washer," add water, a drop of soap liquid, and shake vigorously! How might children apply the same idea to the rinsing process?

Identifying Sounds
Enlist children's help to record sounds of machines such as a hair dryer, typewriter, wind-up clock, or pencil sharpener. If possible, include sounds from some broken machines. Then replay the sounds for children to identify each.

Identifying Machines at Home
Encourage children to ask family members to help make a list of machines at home that use electricity and who would repair each machine. Suggest the use of catalogs and newspapers to include pictures of the machines.

Using Sound Words
Help children speak in sentences to tell about more things that make clicking sounds. Examples might be a key in a lock, a light switch, or a heel on a hard floor. Repeat for more examples of onomotopoeia (words borrowed from sounds), such as *buzz, splash, crack,* or *bang.*

Share more noisy poems such as "Ears Hear," "POP! POPPITY! POP!," "Subway," and "Boom! Bang!" (all in Related Read-Alouds) or read from Jill Bennett's collection, *Noisy Poems.*

Inventing Noisy Machines
Provide new and recycled materials for children to create "noisy machines." Children can tell what their machines do and record the sounds they'd make when they work properly or are broken. Invite children to share their inventions at home.

Our Washing Machine

Our washing machine went whisity whirr

Whisity whisity whisity whirr

One day at noon it went whisity click

Whisity whisity whisity click

Click grr click grr click grr click

    Call the repairman

    Fix it. . .Quick!

Patricia Hubbell

"Our Washing Machine" reprinted with permission of Atheneum Publishers, an imprint of Macmillan Publishing Company, from THE APPLE VENDOR'S FAIR by Patricia Hubbell. Copyright 1963, and renewed 1991, by Patricia Hubbell.

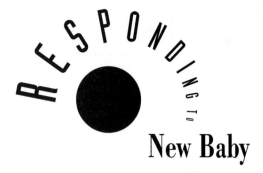

New Baby

by MARY CARTER SMITH

Introducing the Poem

Display the poster and help children recognize that the mother in the illustration is going to have a baby. Read the poem's title and ask children to listen to the poem to find out what the child already knows and doesn't yet know about the new baby. Encourage children to share experiences they've had with new babies in their families.

Sensing a Ticking Heart

Help children place their pointer and middle fingers on their necks or wrists to feel their own pulse. Some children may want to feel your pulse or a friend's. Invite a doctor or nurse to share a stethoscope for children to hear their hearts ticking. Share "Heart Beats" (Related Read-Alouds).

Sharing Feelings

Ask why the child in the poem would feel glad to be getting a new brother or sister. Focus on positive feelings about new babies by sharing Jan Omerod's *101 Things to Do with a Baby* or Frieda Wishenski's *Oonga, Boonga*. Help children recognize that it's okay to have negative feelings about a new baby by sharing Joe Scruggs' recording, "New Baby," and reading books such as *Peter's Chair* by Ezra Jack Keats or Martha Alexander's books, *Nobody Asked Me if I Wanted a Baby Sister* and *When the New Baby Comes, I'm Moving Out*. Children who are adjusting to a new baby will appreciate Mildred Pitts Walter's *My Mama Needs Me*.

Learning about Marsupials

Discuss how humans and marsupials, such as the kangaroo, koala, wombat, and opossum, carry their babies inside their bodies until the babies are born. Share "Secret" (Related Read-Alouds) and then compare how marsupials and humans carry their new babies around.

Drawing Family Portraits

Invite children to draw themselves and other members of their families. Help children write family members' names and use complete sentences such as "This is my big brother, Nate. I like his friends" to "introduce" their family members to classmates and tell something they like about each person. Children will enjoy sharing their portraits with family members.

Taking a Survey

Help children make tallies to count the number of babies in all their families. You might also take surveys to find out how many children are the oldest, youngest, or only child in the family, or count older and younger sisters and brothers. Children without siblings will especially enjoy Marlene Fanta Sheyer's *Here I Am, An Only Child*.

Growing Bigger and Bigger

Invite children to curl up to be as small as possible. Remind children they were even tinier than this when they were new babies. Read "I Am Growing!" (Related Read-Alouds) as children slowly stretch out.

Making Size Comparisons

Draw around children's bodies on butcher paper. Then have children curl up on their outlines to see how much bigger they are now than when they were babies.

Draw and cut out a baby-sized foot or hand. Help children draw around their feet or hands and then see how many of the baby prints fit inside their own.

Have children ask family members to help them compare their present heights, weights, and the current sizes of their feet and hands to their sizes as newborns.

Meeting Babies

Have children invite family members to bring baby siblings to visit the classroom. Share "Moochie" and "Peek-a-boo" (both in Related Read-Alouds) as children plan an activity or two to entertain the babies.

42

New Baby

I'm so glad there'll be another
Maybe sister, maybe brother
Until it's ready to be born
It's inside Mama keeping warm
Doctor says its heart is ticking
Mama let me feel it kicking

Mary Carter Smith

"New Baby" by Mary Carter Smith.
Reprinted by permission of the author.

Dinner Time

by LESLIE D. PERKINS

Enjoying the Poem

Display the poster and ask the time of day and which meal the child is eating. Some children may ask to substitute "supper" for "dinner." After several readings, you might prepare flannelboard pictures for children to tell the poem's story in their own words.

Acting Out Word Meanings

Talk about having a *full* tummy, or feeling stuffed, and a *full* or whole moon. Invite children to form circles with their arms and playact having a full tummy. Share Margaret Hillert's poem about feeling stuffed in "Thanksgiving" (Related Read-Alouds). Then discuss and act out the meanings of other homographs such as *bat* (animal/sports equipment), *bark* (dog's sound/part of tree), *duck* (animal/ bend down to avoid), or *pen* (cage, writing tool).

Charting Food Likes

Help children make a chart and record tallies to show how many of them like to eat rice, beans, or chicken pie.

Rice	✔	✔	✔							
Beans	✔	✔								
Chicken Pie	✔	✔	✔	✔	✔					

Count the tallies to find the most and least favorite foods. Introduce or review "Toy Tik Ka" (Related Read-Alouds).

You may want to make a chart that shows the dinner times of children's families.

Celebrating a Full Moon

Help children note on the calendar when the moon will be full. Build anticipation for the event by displaying a large moon the children paint and cut out. Refer to it as you innovate on the poem's text at snack time. Read Margaret Wise Brown's *Goodnight Moon* and revisit the book's language each day before dismissal. Then enjoy Frank Asch's *Happy Birthday, Moon* when the full moon appears.

Filling Dinner Plates

Provide paper plates, rice, and beans. Help children draw lines on the plates to make three sections. Children can spread glue on two sections, sprinkle rice on one and beans on the other, and then draw and color or cut and glue a circle in the third section to depict chicken pie.

Have children use their "dinner plates" and a large paper moon to present the poem for family members and friends.

Sharing Favorite Foods

Provide magazines and food labels for children to cut out pictures of dinner foods they like. Help children substitute foods such as "potatoes, corn, and pizza pie" for the poem's "rice and beans and chicken pie." Children might glue their pictures on paper plates to share at home or make a class collage titled "It's Dinner Time!"

Identifying Full and Half Moons

Play a variation of "I Spy" for children to identify full circles and half circles like a full or half moon. Players might say, "I spy a full moon on the clock face" or place a sheet of paper over half of a paper plate and say, "I spy a half moon on this plate."

Making "r-Ice" Cubes

Make rice cereal marshmallow treats and cut into cubes to resemble ice cubes. Children will enjoy your playful language as you write and say, "Br-r-r-r-Ice Cubes!" Then you might say, "These aren't br-r-r-r-ice cubes made by freezing water! These are cubes of rice cereal and they're not br-r-r cold! We'll have to erase the br-r-r to have *rice* cubes, not *ice* cubes!"

Matching by Color, Size, and Shape

Provide small containers, each filled with a different type of beans or rice. Glue samples on cards and have children match each container's contents to its sample.

Dinner Time

My dinner's done.
I ate it all–
My rice and beans
And chicken pie.

I look outside
And see the moon–
The moon is full
And so am I!

Leslie D. Perkins

"Dinner Time" by Leslie D. Perkins.
Used by permission of the author.

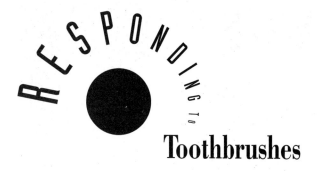

Toothbrushes

by ANONYMOUS

Introducing the Poem
Display the poster and read the poem's title. Help children count the toothbrushes in the illustration and tell the color of each. Ask children to listen to the poem to find out who owns each toothbrush.

Surveying Toothbrush Colors
Make a bar graph to show the colors of the children's own toothbrushes. Children can glue a colored square of paper, or color a square, to represent each brush. Help children identify the longest and shortest bars on the graph and tell what each means.

Have children ask for help at home to list family members' names and the color of each person's toothbrush. Ask children to bring the list to school to use in making a picture. Invite children to paint popsicle sticks the colors of all family members' brushes—including their own! Attach self-adhering strips or pieces of pipe cleaners stuck in clay for the brush. Children might dictate their family members' names or new versions of the poem to accompany their row of brushes mounted on heavy paper. Encourage children to display their pictures in their bathroooms at home.

Matching One to One
Help children use magazines to find pictures of smiling people. Cut out the faces or just the mouths and display them on chart paper or a bulletin board. Invite children to draw or make a toothbrush for each mouth.

Innovating on the Text
Children use the language of literature in their own thinking and talking when they hear you model innovations, such as "Three paint smocks hang in a neat little line..." or "Three school bags lie in a neat little row..."

Learning about Dental Hygiene
Read Fred Rogers' *Going to the Dentist*. If possible, visit a dentist's office or invite a dentist or hygienist to visit the classroom. Before a visit, you might help children list questions they'd like to ask. After a visit, children might make a chart that shows foods that help build strong teeth. Children might give the chart to the dentist or hygienist along with a thank-you note.

Singing about Brushing
Toothbrushes and floss might be donated by a local dentist office for classroom use. Children can make up stanzas about putting toothpaste on the brush, brushing, rinsing the mouth, hanging the toothbrush, and flossing to sing to the tune of "Mulberry Bush" or sing along with Cathy Fink's recording, "Brush Your Teeth."

Identifying All Sorts of Brushes
Provide brushes such as a bottle brush, assorted scrub brushes and hairbrushes, a nail brush, a pet brush, shoe or clothing brush, and a vegetable brush. Help children compare the sizes of the brushes and the textures and lengths of their bristles. Discuss and dramatize the use of each brush and invite children's ideas for inventive uses. Encourage critical thinking by asking questions such as why a wide floor scrubbing brush could not be used to clean a baby's bottle. Suggest that children ask family members to help them look for different kinds of brushes at home and talk about how they use each.

Enjoying Related Literature
Share "This Tooth" (Related Read-Alouds), *Arthur's Tooth* by Marc Brown, *Doctor Desoto* by William Steig, and Nurit Karlin's *The Tooth Witch*.

See Meet the Poets, page 192.

Toothbrushes

Three toothbrushes hang in a neat little line.

We can tell one from another.

The blue one is Gram's.

The red one is mine.

And the green one belongs to my mother.

Anonymous

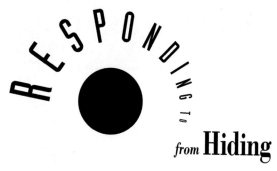

RESPONDING To

from Hiding

by DOROTHY ALDIS

Introducing the Poem

To help children realize that print is "talk written down," dramatize the poster poem before sharing the poster. Stand behind a cupboard door or use a blanket to hide all but your hair and toes as you recite. Invite volunteers to hide and join you in saying the lines.

Once children are familiar with the poem, display the poster and encourage everyone to recite the poem with you to tell what the hidden child in the illustration is saying.

Enjoying More of the Poet's Words

Refer to the poster and ask children who they think the child is hiding from and what they think the dad and mom might be saying. Invite children to listen for their ideas as you read the whole poem. Groups of three might take turns playing the characters as you reread the poem or play the recording.

Writing with Quills

Reread the third stanza and then show children an ink pen. Explain that before pens were invented, people wrote with quills dipped in a container of ink. Provide cups of paint and feathers or popsicle sticks and help children write their names. Encourage children to take their feathers home and invite family members to help them write with paint or ketchup.

Thinking Logically

Ask why Benny could not really hide in an inkwell or a mirror. Help children use the illustration to suggest other places Benny could not possibly hide.

Playing Hiding Games

Invite a volunteer to be the "Sardine" who hides. As others find Sardine, they join Sardine in the hiding place until the last one to find everyone becomes the new Sardine.

Have children take turns hiding an object in one hand for partners to guess which hand it is in.

Hide an object while one child is not looking. Invite others to give clues about the object's location by saying "hot" or "cold" as the "hunter" moves closer to it or farther away.

Learning about Camouflage

Talk about how animals hide to protect themselves or stalk their prey. Share pictures of animals, such as a lizard, chameleon, or praying mantis and talk about how camouflage helps each animal, especially when it sleeps. Challenge children to find the octopus and snow leopard in Eve B. Feldman's *Animals Don't Wear Pajamas*.

Exploring Books about Hiding

Animals play hide and seek in Pat Hutchins' *What Game Shall We Play?* A mother duck searches for her duckling who's hiding in the scenic background in Nancy Tafuri's *Have You Seen My Duckling?* Children love to search for the bespectacled character in Martin Handford's *Waldo* series and find every Goldbug in Richard Scarry's *Cars and Trucks and Things That Go*.

Making Hidden Pictures

Help children camouflage paper circles, rectangles, triangles, diamonds, and squares in a collage of assorted pictures from magazines.

Provide crayons and matching colored paper for children to draw pictures. Cover the drawings with thin white paint and watch the pictures appear!

Enjoying Related Literature

Dramatize searching for the parrot while listening to Hap Palmer's song, "Percival the Parrot." Share Grimms' *Rumpelstiltskin* and talk about what the elf and princess hide from each other. Read *Where's Spot* by Eric Hill, and "Keziah," "Moochie," and "Peek-a-boo" (all in Related Read-Alouds).

Hiding

I'm hiding, I'm hiding,
And no one knows where;
For all they can see is my
    Toes and my hair.

And I just heard my father
Say to my mother—
"But, darling, he must be
    Somewhere or other.

"Have you looked in the inkwell?"
And Mother said, "Where?"
"In the inkwell," said Father. But
    I was not there.

Then "Wait!" cried my mother—
"I think that I see
Him under the carpet." But
    It was not me.

"Inside the mirror's
A pretty good place,"
Said Father and looked, but saw
    Only his face.

"We've hunted," sighed Mother,
"As hard as we could
And I am so afraid that we've
    Lost him for good."

Then I laughed out loud
And I wiggled my toes
And Father said—"Look, dear,
    I wonder if those

"Toes could be Benny's.
There are ten of them. See?"
And they were so surprised to find
    Out it was me!

Dorothy Aldis

"Hiding" by Dorothy Aldis reprinted by permission of G.P. Putnam's Sons
from EVERYTHING AND ANYTHING by Dorothy Aldis, copyright 1925,
1926, 1927, copyright renewed 1953, 1954, 1955 by Dorothy Aldis.

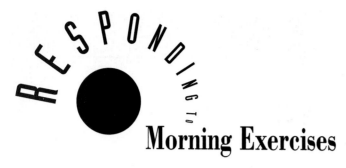

Morning Exercises

by BABS BELL HAJDUSIEWICZ

Introducing the Poem
Display the printless poster and invite discussion about the illustration. Read the poem's title and ask children to listen to the poem to see who is waking up to do morning exercises.

Enjoying a Fingerplay
Children might sit or lie on the floor with thumbs folded inside fists as if the fingers are fast asleep. Index fingers can pop up on cue and then bend and stretch as if doing exercises. Repeat for the other fingers and thumbs. When all fingers have "awakened," children can rub their eyes, pretend to throw off bed covers, and use all ten fingers to push themselves off the floor. Share "Covers," "Night Bear," and read or sing more fingerplays, "Sleepy Fingers," "Fingerplay," and "Thumb Says"(all in Related Read-Alouds). Compare the name variations for fingers to people's given names and nicknames.

Singing the Poem
Children might play the characters' roles as they sing along with the recording. Encourage children to share the song when they wake up at home.

Making Handprints
Invite children to make handprints in sand or clay, make prints using paints, or draw around their hands. Lay out finished handprints for children to find those that match their own hands or find all the left or right handprints.

Use children's handprints to make personalized greeting cards, or glue or sew fabric handprints onto plain hand towels.

Fingerprinting Fingers
Provide paper and help children draw around their hands. Then have children use a stamp pad to place their fingerprints on their handprints. Encourage children to share their pictures with family members.

At other times, compare thumbprints to prints made by index or pinky fingers. Extend children's interests in fingerprints to evaluate their understanding of finger names, position words, shapes, or number values. For example, children might make two pinky prints on or above a line, one thumbprint inside a circle, and so on.

Personalizing the Poem
Children will enjoy hearing their own names in the poem as you model substitutions such as "James and Marcy" for "Pointer Fingers." Have children pretend to be asleep as you read or sing the first stanza. When they hear their names, children can stretch, bend, and say, "We'll do our morning exercises!" Invite ideas for adapting the last stanza.

Making Finger Puppets
Use eyebrow pencil to draw faces on children's fingers or on sticky dots placed on fingertips. Children can have their finger puppets act out the poem.

Share Amy Ehrlich's retelling of Hans Christian Anderson's *Thumbelina* and invite children to use their puppets to act out the story.

Sensing the Morning
Share the recording, "When Ducks Get Up in the Morning," Susan Hellard's *Time to Get Up*, and Nancy White Carlstrom's poetic book, *Wild Wild Sunflower Child Anna*. Have children describe sounds they hear and aromas they smell in the mornings.

Visit a nursery to see and smell morning glory plants. Children might bring back some seeds to plant.

Identifying First, Next, and Last
Have children describe their routine after waking up this morning. What did they do first, next, and last before leaving home to come to school?

Help children form a line and tell who is first, next, and last. Have everyone turn around and tell their new places in line.

See Adding Music, page 175.

See Meet the Poets, page 189.

Morning Exercises

Everyone was fast asleep, all snuggled in their beds,
Until the sun sang out to them, "Wake up, you sleepy heads!"

Pointer Fingers woke up first and jumped right out of bed.
"We'll do our morning exercises!" Pointer Fingers said.

Middle Fingers woke up next and jumped right out of bed.
"We'll do our morning exercises!" Middle Fingers said.

Ringer Fingers woke up next and jumped right out of bed.
"We'll do our morning exercises!" Ringer Fingers said.

Pinky Fingers woke up next and jumped right out of bed.
"We'll do our morning exercises!" Pinky Fingers said.

Sleepy Thumbers woke up last and jumped right out of bed.
"We'll do our morning exercises!" Sleepy Thumbers said.

When everyone was wide awake, they rubbed my eyes and said,
"Come on, wake up, you sleepy head! We'll pull you out of bed!"

Babs Bell Hajdusiewicz

"Morning Exercises" © 1992 by Babs Bell
Hajdusiewicz. Used by permission of the author.

Grandpa

by JEAN PARKER KATZ

Talking about the Picture

Display the poster and invite discussion around ideas in the illustration that are obvious and ideas that might be implied, such as the relationship between the people, why they're working together, or how each is feeling. Encourage children to tell about adults who are special to them and the kinds of activities they do together.

Enjoying the Poem

Ask children to listen to the poem to find out who is talking. Reread the poem and invite children's ideas about how the girl feels about her grandpa and why, where the grandpa lives, or what the girl and her grandpa might do next.

Learning about Grandpas

Discuss more kinds of activities a grandpa and grandchild might do together and other ways a grandpa might help a child. Talk about ways we show respect for a grandpa or other older person, such as being helpful or asking for advice.

Read "Gramps and I" (Related Read-Alouds), Patricia MacLachlan's *Through Grandpa's Eyes*, Tommie de Paola's *Now One Foot, Now the Other*, or Amy Hest's books, *The Crack-of-Dawn Walkers* and *The Purple Coat*.

You may want to invite a senior citizen to spend time in your classroom or even adopt a "class grandpa" for children to have experiences with a loving older adult.

Making a Life-Size "Grandpa"

Help children stuff old clothes with pillows or rags to make a life-size grandpa figure. Facial features might be painted or glued on a small pillow held in place by a broom or dowel rod. Children can name "Grandpa" and include him in special activities, curl up beside him to read or rest, or share him with another class or with family members at home.

Recording "Grandpa" Messages

Invite children to tell what they'd like a grandpa to say to them and then pretend to be a grandpa who says those words using their very own names! Remind children to use their "grandpa" voices as you record the messages. Replay children's words and then set the tape aside for the next activity when everyone goes to "visit Grandpa."

Going to Visit "Grandpa"

Remove the grandpa figure before children arrive one day. In "Grandpa's" place might be a letter from him that explains his temporary absence and includes a map and an invitation to come visit him at his "house." Help children follow the map from the classroom to "Grandpa's House," a place in the building where "Grandpa" is waiting for them. "Grandpa" can greet children via the recorded messages suggested in the activity above.

Innovating on the Text

Share *Me and Nana* by Leslie Kimmelman and then use a sticky tab to substitute the letter *m* for *p* in the poster poem's title. Read the new title and reread the poem as you help children notice that *Grandpa*, *he,* and perhaps other words need to be changed for their new poem to make sense.

At other times, you might substitute titles such as *Sister, Gramps, Granny,* or other special names. Children will enjoy dictating personalized versions of the poem to give to special people in their lives.

Role-Playing a Grandparent

Invite individuals to be "Grandpa" or "Grandma" for a day and wear a special name tag planned and created by the children. The grandparent's role might focus on "being there to help" fasten a shoe, read a book, give advice, or offer a hug. Others might show their respect and appreciation by reserving first place in line for the honoree, asking for help, sharing, or by providing comforts such as fetching the "grandparent's" coat.

Grandpa

Grandpa takes me to the park
And sometimes to the zoo,
But even when we stay at home
We've lots of things to do.

He shows me how to hammer nails
And helps me climb a tree.
I love my grandpa!
He's my friend.
He likes to be with me.

Jean Parker Katz

"Grandpa" by Jean Parker Katz.
Used by permission of the author.

In the Tub

by LADA JOSEFA KRATKY

Setting the Stage
Read Matt Faulkner's *The Amazing Voyage of Jackie Grace* and play the Sesame Street recording of "Rubber Duckie." Encourage children to tell about games they like to play in their bathtubs at home.

Introducing the Poem
Display the poster and read the poem's title. Have children listen to the poem to name two kinds of animals the child pretends to be in the tub. Share pictures of a whale and trout and help children compare the animals' sizes.

Blowing Whale-Size Bubbles
Remove the tops and bottoms of three soup cans and help children tape them together to make a super bubble blower. Make a bubble solution by mixing one quart of warm water and one quarter cup liquid soap. Encourage children to describe their bubbles.

Identifying Spouts
Talk about how the whale *spouts* water from its blowhole. Then help children name other kinds of spouts, such as a spout, faucet, or spigot on a drinking fountain, sink, sprinkling can, or teapot. Encourage children to invite family members to go on a water spout hunt with them at home. Children will also enjoy dramatizing and singing "I'm a Little Teapot."

Identifying Water Animals
Help children name more animals that live in water. Examples might include a snail, turtle, shark, dolphin, jellyfish, octopus, and catfish. Share Peter Seymour's pop-up book, *What's in the Deep Blue Sea?*

Wiggling and Waggling
Ask children to show how a whale might wiggle and waggle. Then invite children to wiggle or waggle one shoulder, the other shoulder, and then both. Repeat for one toe, the right knee, and so on. Share Hap Palmer's recording, "Wiggy Wiggy Wiggles."

Listening for Rhyming Sounds
Ask children to listen to the poem and wiggle like a whale each time they hear a word that rhymes with *spout* (about, trout, trout, out). Repeat to identify rhyming words in other poems such as "After a Bath" or "Bubble Trouble?" (both in Related Read-Alouds).

Children might think of things they do in the tub that rhyme with *tub*. Examples may be *scrub, rub, rub-a-dub-dub* or submerge like a *sub*.

Finding What Floats or Sinks
Set out a container filled with about four inches of water. Provide objects such as a cork, plastic lid, pencil, and pieces of cardboard, bark, driftwood, foam, grass, or paper. Invite children to predict which will float or sink and then test their predictions.

Pretending to Take a Bath
Invite children to join in as you pretend to take a bath. Innovate on "The Mulberry Bush" to sing, "This is the way I wash my nose," and so on.

Children love to sit in a large box and pretend to take a bath. You may want to provide a doll for children to pretend or actually give "the baby" a bath. Encourage talk about testing the water to see if it's too hot, too cold, or just right.

Share Pam Conrad's *Tub People*, Barbro Lindgren's *Sam's Bath*, or Kevin Henkes' *Clean Enough*.

Viewing Water's Effect
To help children see how water distorts the appearance of objects, stand a pencil in a clear glass that's half full of water. Repeat for a penny or other small object. You may want to use a larger container of water for children to experience the water's effect on their perspective as they try to retrieve an object that's underwater.

In the Tub

I swim and spout
and wave my tail
in the tub–
I am a whale.
I wiggle and waggle
and swish about
in the tu–
I am a trout.

But spouting whale
and wiggling trout
turn into ME
when I jump out!

Lada Josefa Kratky

"In the Tub" by Lada Josefa Kratky.
Used by permission of the author.

Community

Unit 3

1. Chucka-chucka Choo-choo

2. Gobble! Gobble! Munch!

3. Signs

4. two friends

5. Shopping Day

6. My Friends

7. I'm Sharing

8. Streets

Glug! Gurgle! Glug!

by BABS BELL HAJDUSIEWICZ

Building on Prior Knowledge

Help children talk about how food goes into a person's stomach and then provides energy. Discuss how vehicles have gasoline tanks that hold gasoline to give the vehicles energy. You might extend the analogy to talk about how people have little energy when they're hungry just like a car cannot go when it's "hungry" or has an empty gas tank. Children who have been in a car that has run out of gas might describe how a car jerks and makes sounds when it's out of gas.

Enjoying a Hand Rhyme

Children will want to join in on the first reading and make the hand motions you model. Pretend a fist is the gas tank and an index finger is the gas nozzle. Move your hand up and down for the car's motion, make jerky movements for the car's sputtering, and look puzzled about what is wrong. When children are familiar with the poem, add music to sing the words or play the recorded song for children to join in.

Dramatizing the Poem

Use toy or clay cars to act out the poem, or have children play the roles of cars or hold pieces of yarn or hose to be gas pumps.

You may want to evaluate children's understanding of position words as they act out the poem.

At snack time, try adapting the poem's language to say or sing, "The bites of food go into my mouth. Chew! Chewy! Chew!" Encourage children to ask family members at home to help substitute words in the poem to describe a pet's eating habits.

Making "Gas Pumps"

Children can write numbers on paper rectangles and tape the "gauges" onto "pumps" that are blocks of wood, play bricks, or recycled milk cartons. Use yarn "hoses" with recycled crayons as nozzles.

Imitating Vehicle Sounds

Encourage children to imitate sounds that vehicles make, such as the start-up whirr of an engine, windshield wipers' swishing, the whoosh of air brakes on a semi truck, or the squeal of tires on pavement.

Exploring Full and Empty

Model the use of words such as *empty, full, almost, nearly,* and *half* as children transfer water or sand between various-sized containers. Fill a sink with water and pull the plug, or provide containers and a meat baster or hose, if possible, for children to hear actual "glug" sounds.

Enjoying Related Literature

Introduce or review "Signs" and "Streets" (Community: Posters 3 and 8). Read Anne Rockwell's books about vehicles and Richard Scarry's *Cars and Trucks and Things that Go.* Share "One for Me," "Where's My Seat Belt?" and "Alas!" (all in Related Read-Alouds).

Activity Page 5: Fill It Up and Go!

Reproduce the page and have children cut out the car playing pieces. Cut out and shuffle the sixteen shape cards and two sad cars and lay them face down in a pile. Tell children to "fill up" at the gas station to start the game. Players take turns drawing cards and moving to the next indicated shape. Drawing a sad car sends the driver back to the gas station to refuel and begin again. The first player to return to the station wins.

Activity Page 6: The Gas Station

Discuss the kinds of services, such as a car wash, gas, air for tires, and engine repair, that are available at gas stations. Reproduce the page and have children cut out the pictures at the bottom. Challenge children to place each car in the area of the gas station where it can get the help it needs.

See Meet the Poets, page 189.

See Adding Music, page 170.

Glug! Gurgle! Glug!

The gasoline goes into my car.
Glug!
Gurgle!
Glug!
It makes my car go very far.
Glug!
Gurgle!
Glug!
Uphill,
Downhill,
Up and down.
Uphill,
Downhill,
Up and down.
But suddenly my car won't go!
Sputter!
Sputter!
Sput!
What is wrong?
I do not know!
Sputter!
Sputter!
Sput!
The other cars around me pass.

Sputter!
Sputter!
Sput!
Ah! I think my car is out of gas!
Sputter!
Sputter!
Sput!
The gasoline goes into my car.
Glug!
Gurgle!
Glug!
It makes my car go very far.
Glug!
Gurgle!
Glug!
Uphill,
Downhill,
Up and down.
Uphill,
Downhill,
Up and down.

Babs Bell Hajdusiewicz

Fill It Up and Go!

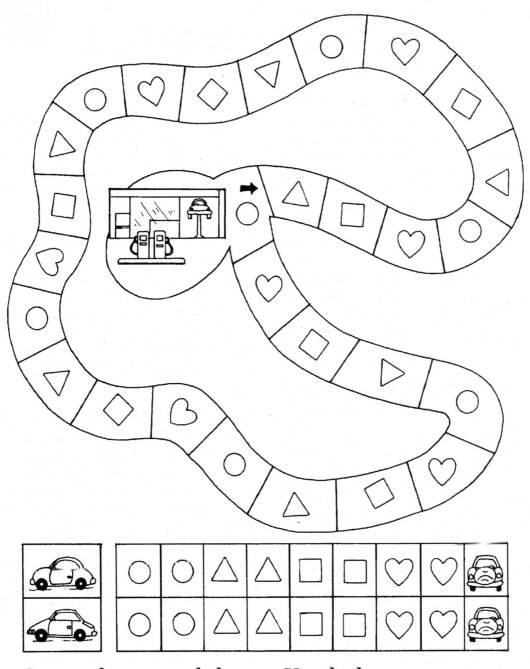

Cut out the cars and shapes. Use the large cars as playing pieces. Place the shape cards and the sad cars upside down to use as a draw pile. Draw a card and move to the next space that has the same shape. If you draw a sad car, return to the gas station.

Activity Page 6: Glug! Gurgle! Glug!

The Gas Station

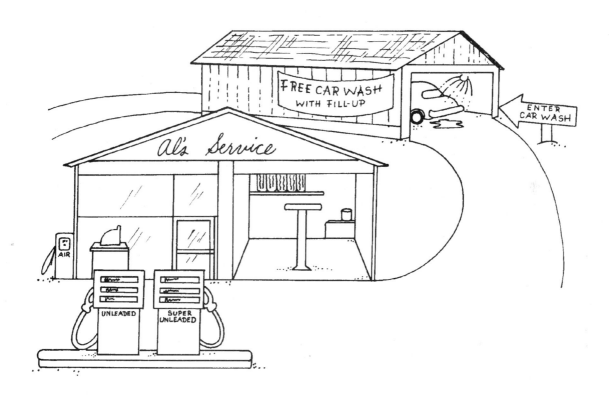

Cut out the pictures and park each car in the part of the gas station where it can get the help it needs.

Chucka-chucka Choo-choo

by SUNDAIRA MORNINGHOUSE

Listening to Identify Sounds

Ask children to listen to identify the sounds at the beginning of the recorded poem. Stop the tape after the whistle sounds and encourage discussion about children's experiences with real and toy trains. Invite children to imitate train sounds.

Introducing the Poem

Display the poem poster and ask children to predict the kinds of sound words and the color word they might hear in this poem. You may want to use a toy train or a train picture to act out the poem as you read or as children listen to the recording.

Focus on sound words by modeling how words like *Chucka-chucka choo-choo* and *clackety-clack* can be chanted loudly or softly to indicate that the train is near or far away. Children might chant the words or use rhythm instruments to accompany repeated readings of the poem.

Dramatizing the Poem

Invite three or four children to form a line to play-act the train's movements. Help children recognize the need for cooperation as more "boxcars" join in for each repeated reading.

Talk about why and how a train might turn around. Why might additional track be needed? Why might a new locomotive simply replace the caboose?

Learning about Trains

Stimulate thought about the purpose of trains by asking children where they think the train is going and why. Talk about how passenger trains carry people from place to place while freight trains haul goods such as lumber, cars, and grains. Allow time for children to role-play "workers" who guide stuffed animals into "passenger cars"

or "load" real or imaginary items onto "boxcars." Encourage children to watch for trains in their neighborhoods to see what each carries.

Talk about how wheels allow train cars to move along a track. Sing "Wheels on the Bus" substituting the appropriate words about trains. Children will enjoy naming the kinds of cars and the color of each in Donald Crews' *Freight Train*.

Comparing Weights

Provide materials such as torn newspaper, marbles, rice, and blocks along with equal-size containers such as milk cartons cut to resemble boxcars. Before children fill the containers, encourage predictions that compare the heaviness of a "boxcar" of marbles to that of other loads. Children might arrange their boxcar loads from lightest to heaviest.

Experimenting with Energy

Remind children that people need food for energy to work and play. Then talk about a train's use of oil, coal, or electricity for energy. Children will enjoy forming a "train" and carrying backpacks or bags to experience using more effort and energy to haul heavier loads. If possible, have the train go up a ramp or hill.

This is a good time to read *The Little Engine That Could* by Watty Piper. You may also want to focus on a car's use of gasoline in "Glug! Gurgle! Glug!" (Community: Theme Opener).

Making a Train

Invite children to work cooperatively to make a train using containers such as milk cartons or cereal boxes. Provide thread spools or large buttons for wheels and yarn or twist ties for train car connectors. Ask children to place drawn or cut-out pictures in their train cars to show what each carries.

Enjoying More Train Poems

Children will enjoy acting out "Boxcars," "Subway," and "El Train," or adding music to sing "The Train" (all in Related Read-Alouds). Children might perform all the train poems for family members and friends.

See Meet the Poet, page 190.

Chucka-chucka Choo-choo

Chucka-chucka choo-choo
where are you going to to
red train on the railroad track
wheels a-going
clackety-clack
clackety-clackety-clackety clack

Chucka-chucka choo-choo
I am going through through
city city
town and town
pick up a load
then turn around
clackety-clack clackety-clack
clackety-clackety-clackety clack

Sundaira Morninghouse

"Chucka-chucka Choo-choo" by Sundaira
Morninghouse. Reprinted by permission of
Carletta Wilson.

Gobble! Gobble! Munch!

by BABS BELL HAJDUSIEWICZ

Making Predictions
Before displaying the poster, emphasize the rhythm as you chant, "Gobble! Gobble! Munch!" Ask children who they think might make those sounds or say words like that.

At another time, compare another "Gobble! Gobble!" in "Turkey Gobbler" (Related Read-Alouds).

Introducing the Poem
Have children listen to the poem to find out who is speaking and to whom. Encourage children to join in on the repetitive lines as you chant the poem dramatically. Display the poster for successive readings and invite children to move their hands to look like the truck's mouth.

Identifying and Classifying
Using real objects or flannelboard pictures, help children identify items the garbage truck in the poem would and would not like for lunch. Children might place the items under YES and NO labels or sort items to show which are paper, plastic, glass, or metal products.

Encourage explorations at school and at home to identify more things the garbage truck would or would not want to eat.

Learning about Recycling
Help children recognize that even though garbage trucks can't really talk, they might say this poem's words if they could. Include words like recycle and reuse to discuss how cans can be crushed, melted, and made into new cans, how egg shells and banana peels are biodegradable because they break up and give food back to the soil, or how paper can be reused.

Share The World that Jack Built by Ruth Brown, Where Does the Garbage Go? by Paul Showers, Tom Chapin's song, "Good Garbage," or Rosenshotz's "Garbage."

Reading Chorally
Invite small groups or individual children to be "garbage trucks" who recite particular lines as others accompany them with a soft chant of "Gobble! Gobble! Munch!"

Help children paint paper bag costumes or use toy trucks and change street, me, I, and this to their plural forms to present the poem as an ecological message to family members and friends.

Building Vocabulary
Identify garbage, trash and waste as words that mean the same thing, and then explore uses of the words such as in trash can, waste basket, trash basket, garbage disposal, or garbage dump.

Using and Reusing
Provide newspapers and help each child find a letter, word, or picture of interest. Share "Yesterday's Paper" (Related Read-Alouds) to introduce the idea of reusing papers. Then help children think of ways to reuse their papers at school or at home. Ideas might include cutting out letters to make name tags, making a bed for a pet, wrapping a present, or protecting something or someone against wetness or cold or dirt. Children might illustrate their reuses and then tell their pictures' stories to classmates.

Innovating on the Text
Using puppets or pictures, model changing words in the poem's last line. A rabbit, for example, might say, "What will you be serving for this bunny rabbit's lunch?" while a boy might say, "What will you be serving this hungry boy for lunch?" Help children change words in the other stanzas to show that different characters are speaking.

At other times, model innovations that suggest a tummy's asking for nutritious foods instead of junk foods or a dinner guest's saying, "PLEASE serve me...." Children will enjoy personalizing the poem to state their food preferences to family members at home.

See Meet the Poet, page 189.

Gobble! Gobble! Munch!

Gobble, gobble, munch!
Gobble, gobble, munch!
What will you be serving
on your street for lunch?

Don't serve me paper!
Don't serve me cans!
Don't serve me metal
or aluminum pans!

Don't serve me plastic!
Don't serve me glass!
I would rather munch on
egg shells or grass.

Gobble, gobble, munch!
Gobble, gobble, munch!
What will you be serving
this garbage truck for lunch?

Babs Bell Hajdusiewicz

RESPONDING to

Signs

by LOUISE BINDER SCOTT

Setting the Stage

Display the poster in a prominent spot in the classroom several days prior to introducing the poem. Meanwhile, take every opportunity to point out signs that help you and the children with comments such as, "There's a *sign* that tells us...."

Giving Meaning to Print

Point to the appropriate sign in the illustration as you read the poem aloud. Encourage children to join in on the repeated words. On a second reading, track the words and have volunteers find each sign.

Identifying Shapes and Colors

Help children tell the color, shape, and number of sides of each sign in the poster's illustration. Invite children to use toothpicks and miniature marshmallows to make some of the signs' shapes. Share any of Tana Hoban's books about shapes, signs, and symbols.

Telling Why Signs Are Helpful

Reread each line of the poem for children to tell ways each sign helps people. For example, when a painter paints a park bench, how does a "Wet Paint" sign help both the painter and a runner who wants to stop to rest? What might happen if someone doesn't obey a stop sign or doesn't know what a "This way to the zoo" sign means?

Enjoying Related Poems

Introduce "Streets" (Community: Poster 8), "Traffic Light," "City Street," "Stop, Look, Listen," and sing and act out "Stop Sign's Song" (all in Related Read-Alouds). Then invite a child be a "Traffic Light" to hold red and green circles to play "Red Light, Green Light." "Travelers" must watch the "light" and move forward or stop.

Using Traffic Signs

Tape long sheets of paper to the floor to form two or more intersecting "streets." Help children paint white or yellow center lines and draw or glue pictures of houses, stores, and other buildings along each street's sides. Enlarge the sign patterns (See page 272) for children to color and glue onto cardboard. Have children hold the signs to help others who "drive," walk, or maneuver toy vehicles along the streets.

Being "Sign Detectives"

Invite children to go on a sign search through the building or neighborhood. "Sign Detectives" should look for traffic signs and informational signs such as on restroom doors, billboards, stores, or "For Sale" signs. Which signs have pictures? Which have words? Which have both? Help "detectives" interpret each sign and use the poem's pattern to report, "This sign says..." for each "sighting." Encourage children to go on sign searches in their homes and neighborhoods with family members.

Using Signs with Arrows

Draw arrows that point up, down, left, or right on individual sheets of paper. Help children point to and describe the direction each arrow points and then place the arrow signs above, below, or to the right or left of objects to point out the water faucet, pencil sharpener, and so on. Help children use the poem's model to tell about each sign. Or stage a treasure hunt in which children follow a succession of signs with arrows.

Making Helpful Signs

Talk about how name tag signs and signs that identify places and materials in the classroom not only help classmates but also make a visitor or new classmate feel "at home." Then help children discover a need and make a sign that helps themselves and others in the school or classroom.

Signs

This sign says, "Keep off the grass."

This sign says, "Do not pass."

This sign says, "Stop! Light is red."

This sign says, "One lane ahead."

This sign says, "Yellow——slow."

This sign says, "Green light, go."

This sign says, "This paint is new."

This sign says, "This way to the zoo."

Louise Binder Scott

Excerpt of "Signs" from RHYMES FOR LEARNING TIMES by
Louise Binder Scott © 1983 T.S. Denison and Company Inc.
Minneapolis, MN. Reprinted by permission of publisher.

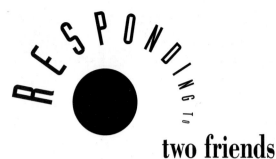

two friends

by NIKKI GIOVANNI

Introducing the Poem
Display the poster and track the words in the title as you read aloud. Track the girls' names and the number words and point out the girls' ears, pigtails, and so on as you read the poem. On the second reading, encourage children to join in to say the number words, show each quantity on their fingers, and identify the girls' items.

Describing Two Friends
Ask children what else might be listed to describe the two friends. Encourage all sorts of ideas such as two noses, two brains, lots of teeth, lots of feelings, and so on.

Take photos of pairs of children and help each pair use the poem's model to tell about their picture as you write their poem. You may stimulate new friendships by focusing solely on what *both* children in the picture have, or what the two have in common.

Learning What Friends Do
Help children think about what makes "one good friendship" by sharing sentences such as, "Good friends play together" or "Good friends share." As children offer more ideas about good friends, encourage thoughts about helping, not making fun of each other, hugging, and even sometimes disagreeing.

Finding Pairs
Point out children's shoes and count, "One, two," for each *pair*. Repeat for pairs of eyes or hands and help children name other things in pairs such as mittens or eyebrows.

Help partners draw around their hands, feet, or shoes on the same piece of paper. Children can write their names to complete a caption such as, "(Name) and (Name) have two pairs of (item)." Make copies for children to share their drawings at home.

Have children draw around their hands and, perhaps, draw a ring on one hand to make take-home Concentration cards. Make an even number of copies for children to match pairs of right or left hands or pairs of hands. Read Bruce McMillan's *One, Two, One Pair* to view twins as examples of pairs.

Dressing Up
Invite pairs of children to dress up and then recall the poem with you to tell about their choices of apparel. Motivate others to describe the dressed-up pairs by starting a sentence such as, "Salim and Amy have one hat, two belts,..." Share Shiego Watanabe's book, *How Do I Put It On?*

Measuring to Make Accessories
Provide yarn and a variety of macaroni noodles for children to make belts, necklaces, and bracelets. Model the use of words like *long, longer, longest, short, shorter,* and *shortest* as you help children wrap yarn around their waists or wrists to approximate lengths needed before cutting.

Enjoying Hats
Read Ann Morris' *Hats, Hats, Hats* and provide various kinds of hats for children to try on. Help children cut pictures from magazines and catalogs or use real hats to make a hat collage titled "Hats, Hats, Hats."

Provide a mirror, a soft, floppy hat with a brim, and a large scarf for children to explore ways to mold or position the hat, wrap and tie the scarf, or combine the two to create hats of a chef, a firefighter, and so on.

Finding Stripes
Help children find stripes in the poster's illustration and then look around for vertical stripes that seem to stand up, horizontal stripes that seem to lie down, and stripes that go round and round on a candy cane or barber's pole. Introduce or review "Tiger" (Animals: Poster 6).

Reading about Friends
Share "from A Friend" (Me: Poster 8) and "My Friends" (Community: Poster 6) along with "Two Little Sisters (Related Read-Alouds), James Marshall's *George and Martha*, Mr. Rogers' *Making Friends*, and Eric Carle's *Do You Want to Be My Friend?*

two friends

lydia and shirley have
two pierced ears and
two bare ones
five pigtails
two pairs of sneakers
two berets
two smiles
one necklace
one bracelet
lots of stripes and
one good friendship

Nikki Giovanni

"two friends" from SPIN A SOFT BLACK SONG by Nikki Giovanni.
Copyright © 1971,1985 by Nikki Giovanni. Reprinted by
permission of Farrar, Straus & Giroux, Inc.

Shopping Day

by BABS BELL HAJDUSIEWICZ

Building On Prior Knowledge

Using words like *produce aisle, dairy aisle, deli,* and *frozen foods section,* tell children about a recent trip of yours to the grocery store. Identify the day on a calendar and tell some of the items you bought. Ask children to tell about their grocery shopping trips.

Introducing the Poem

Encourage discussion about what Tub E. Bear is doing in the printless poster's illustration and why he's holding a piece of paper. Point out the calendar in the picture and ask children to listen to the poem to find out what day Tub E. Bear is shopping and why that day.

Thinking about Shopping

Provide food items or flannelboard pictures for children to identify the listed foods as you reread the poem. How many and what items does Tub E. get in each aisle. What else might be in each aisle? Does Tub E. mark each item off his list? If he lives alone, might Tub E. buy a quart or gallon of milk, a dozen or half dozen eggs? Which costs more? How often might Tub E. need to shop?

Encourage children to consider their family size as it relates to the frequency of shopping trips and quantities purchased.

Making a Shopping List

Provide magazines, package labels, and grocery ads for groups to make pictured shopping lists. One group might list items from the dairy aisle, and so on. You might write food names beside their pictures.

Children might make a shopping list for a class visit to a neighborhood grocery or supermarket or help family members list items they need to remember to buy.

Playing with Words and Sounds

Read aloud as you write *Tub E. Bear* and *Tubby Bear.* Reread both names for children to hear their identical sounds. Help children think of other names such as Fun E. Fox or John E. Giraffe that can be written two ways.

Building Vocabulary

Share books about shopping such as Arnold Lobel's *On Market Street,* Helen Oxenbury's *Shopping Trip,* or *Max and Diana and the Shopping Trip* by Harriet Ziefert. Then use real items or pictures to help children tell the kind of store in which they'd find shoes, toys, bread, a bed or T.V., medicine, or a pet. Ask about shops where people have shoes or watches or cars repaired, rent movies, or get haircuts.

Help children position chairs to create *aisles* to talk about, and dramatize Tub E. Bear's shopping trip, or family visits to the library or video rental store.

Enjoying Rhyme

Reread the poem to help children identify the rhyming words *pay* and *day* or *eggs* and *leg.* Continue for other rhyming words in the poem. Children will enjoy the many rhyming pairs in "Mr. Bear" (Nature: Theme Opener), another poem about another very sleepy bear.

Singing about Shopping

Children can sing the poem's first stanza to the tune of "Twinkle, Twinkle, Little Star."

Invite children to waddle like a bear or duck, slither like a snake, or hop like a kangaroo. Then introduce Hap Palmer's "Sammy," a song about shopping.

Thinking about Bears

Share "In the Summer We Eat" (Related Read-Alouds) and talk about how some bears and other animals store up food before hibernating for the winter. Ask why we might think Tub E. bear is preparing to hibernate. Encourage children to tell how they know that Tub E. Bear is not a real bear. Children will enjoy hearing "Grizzly Bear" (Related Read-Alouds) and telling about bears they've seen at a zoo or circus.

See Meet the Poet, page 189.

Shopping Day

Tub E. Bear just got his pay.
It's Friday, Tub E.'s shopping day.
He checks his grocery list awhile,
Then waddles down the produce aisle
     for lettuce
     apples
     carrots
     beans
     sweet potatoes
     tangerines.
He checks his grocery list awhile
Then waddles down the dairy aisle
     for cheeses
     yogurt
     milk
     and eggs
     Oops! Forgot the chicken legs!
He checks his grocery list awhile
Then waddles down some other aisles
     for peanut butter
     bread
     and rice
     some pretzels
     and a bag of ice.
He gets in line and waits to pay.
It's Friday, Tub E.'s eating day!

Babs Bell Hajdusiewicz

My Friends

by SYDNIE MELTZER KLEINHENZ

Introducing the Poem

Display the poster and read the poem's title. Ask children to listen to the poem to find out who the friends are and what each does. For repeated readings, help children substitute the names of their own neighborhood friends.

Singing about Friends

Track the words on the poster as children listen to the recording or sing along.

Identifying Workers' Titles

Help children use titles such as *mail carrier, firefighter, electrician,* and so on for the workers in the poem. Then have children pantomime doing jobs, or give clues such as "I sell flowers" or "I put out fires" for classmates to guess the worker's title. Share *The Emergency Room* by Harlow Rockwell and "Emergency," "Buy My Flowers," and "Stop, Drop, and Roll" (all in Related Read-Alouds), and "Hot Cross Buns" (Nursery Rhymes: Poster 2).

Recognizing Workers

Talk about how some workers' uniforms, hats, footwear, or tools give clues about the kind of work they do. Take a walk to look for workers who wear special clothing or use special tools for their jobs.

Read "Shoes" (Related Read-Alouds), *Hats, Hats, Hats* by Ann Morris, and *Shoes* by Elizabeth Winthrop. Have children cut out pictures of hats, clothing, and shoes and sort the pictures, tell who might wear each, or draw self-portraits and "try on" the items.

Learning about Work

Discuss the jobs in Eve Merriam's books, *Mommies at Work* and *Daddies at Work*, Michelle Edwards' *Chicken Man*, in "Different People" and "Inside Outside Upside Down" (both in Related Read-Alouds), and talk about workers depicted in Patrick Connor's *People at Work.*

Help children find out about family members' jobs and any special uniforms or equipment they use. Then invite each child to draw a family member at work and dictate a sentence about the person's work. Have children sign and mount their drawings to give to the person.

Being Bagel and Pizza Makers

Spread warm pizza sauce on bagel chips, crackers, or toasted English muffins and add shredded cheese for yummy pizza snacks.

Roll strips of clay and join the ends or punch a hole through the middle of a clay ball to make pretend bagels. Roll out clay pizza "crusts" and add clay toppings, or glue red paper "sauce" on a paper plate and add colored paper pieces as toppings.

Share *Bread, Bread, Bread* by Ann Morris. If possible, take children to visit a bakery or pizza parlor. List questions children would like to ask the baker and record their interview with a new friend.

Identifying Beginning Sounds

Ask children to listen for words that begin with the sound of *b* as you read the poem's first line. Repeat for the sounds of *p, f,* or *s* in other lines. Help children list more words and names that begin with each sound.

Publishing a Personal Book

Invite children to join you to act out "When I Grow Up" (Related Read-Alouds) and then publish the poem as a book to give to family members. Separate the poem's lines and make copies of the pages. Take two photos of each child or use self-portraits for the book's beginning and ending. Children might draw themselves as postal workers, drummers, and so on, or use magazine pictures to illustrate those pages.

See Adding Music, page 177.

My Friends

I'm buddies with the bagel baker.
Pals with Pearl, the pizza maker.
Ronnie brings the mail each day.
Belsky hauls our trash away.
Fonda works at fighting fires.
Mr. Greg repairs the wires.
Sergeant Soto says "Hello."
Friends are everywhere I go.

Sydnie Meltzer Kleinhenz

"My Friends" by Sydnie Meltzer Kleinhenz.
Used by permission.

I'm Sharing

by LADA JOSEFA KRATKY

Introducing the Poem
Display the poster and help children use the illustration and the poem's title to predict what the child is sharing. List the predictions, and then ask children to listen for their ideas as you read the poem aloud.

Telling the Poem's Story
To help children tell the illustration's story in their own words, ask what might have happened earlier, what is happening now, and what might happen next.

Talking about Sharing
Help childen recognize the different ways the child is sharing. For example, a tortilla can be divided into pieces, but what about a bike or a granny? Help children think of strategies for taking turns so everyone gets a fair share. Examples might be tossing a coin to see who goes first, measuring or using a timer to keep shares equal, or making a list much like a jobs list in the classroom. You'll want to commend children when you observe them using their ideas.

Talk about and act out the frustration of waiting for a turn, the joy of getting a turn, and the sad feeling when a turn is over.

Talking about Not Sharing
Encourage children to talk about times they didn't want to share or how they felt when someone else didn't share. Then read *Mine's the Best* by Crosby N. Bonsall, Leo Lionni's *It's Mine*, and "My Teddy" (Related Read-Alouds).

Sharing Ideas and Feelings
Emphasize the word *share* as you invite children to *share* stories about times they've *shared* things. You'll want to take the opportunity to give compliments to listeners and talkers who share by taking turns to talk, by listening attentively, and by telling their ideas and feelings.

This is a good time to model saying "thank you" to the poet and illustrator who have *shared* their ideas and feelings by writing and illustrating this poem. Read "The Poet Says" (Related Read-Alouds), and invite children to draw pictures of themselves sharing a toy with a best friend. Help others say "thank you" as illustrators share their pictures.

Dividing to Share
Children will enjoy Bruce McMillan's *Eating Fractions*. Read Pat Hutchins' *The Doorbell Rang* and dramatize the story using cookies or another food. You might add to the story by providing small cups and a pitcher of water or juice. Allow time for small groups to experiment to find ways to share the food and drinks equally among themselves.

Tasting Bread Products
Read Ann Morris' *Bread, Bread, Bread* about breads enjoyed by people all over the world. Plan a bread-tasting picnic, outside if possible, for children to taste tortillas and other bread products such as pita bread, bagels, crackers, rolls, and rye, pumpernickel, or whole wheat breads.

Building Vocabulary
Help children recognize that someone named *Mike* might also be called *Michael* and *Letisha* might be called *Tish*. Then help children tell other names for *Granny, Manny,* and *bike.* Continue for alternate forms of words like *telephone, plane, gasoline, Mom,* or *TV.* Encourage children to ask family members to help them think of more examples.

Singing Related Songs
Share Raffi's "Sharing Song" and F.M. Griego's song picture book, *Tortilas Paramama.*

I'm Sharing

I'm sharing
my bike,
tortilla,
and Granny
with my best friends,
María and Manny.

Lada Josefa Kratky

"I'm Sharing" by Lada Josefa Kratky.
Used by permission of the author.

Streets

by AILEEN FISHER

Identifying Home Streets

Hold up a strip of gray paper that's marked with a center line and say, "This is my street. I live on (street name)." Invite children to follow your model to tell their streets' names.

You may want to record children's sentences about their street names and then have them listen to the recording to identify their own voices and street names.

Introducing the Poem

Display the poster and read the poem's title. Ask children to listen to find out how the cars go as you read the poem aloud.

For repeated readings, invite children to pretend to be cars that move one by one or two by two around the room. Children might recite with the recording as they move their arms up, down, in, and out like streets.

Building Vocabulary

Use the children's street names to compile a list of words for *street*. Examples might be *avenue, lane, boulevard, highway, drive, place, court, way,* or *parkway.*

Help children use the words *cars, autos,* and *automobiles* interchangeably. Have children name vehicles such as cars, trucks, bicycles, buses, horse-drawn carriages, and trolleys that travel on city streets. Children might also help list brand names of cars or special kinds of trucks such as a dump truck, pick-up, semi-truck or eighteen-wheeler, garbage truck, and so on.

Learning Where Streets Go

Take children outside to explore a street or two around the school. Have children tell where they think a street leads and what buildings, stores, and so on they'd expect to find if they walked there. Then walk the street to check the predictions.

Encourage children to ask family members to walk with them to see where a neighborhood street goes.

Being Safe Riders and Walkers

Use riding toys or have children pretend to be drivers, walkers, and passengers to act out situations that demonstrate why a walker needs to cross at a corner crosswalk and stop at each corner, why drivers of cars might not be able to see walkers, or why it's dangerous to chase a ball into a street. Help drivers and passengers recite "One For Me" or sing "Where's My Seat Belt?" (both in Related Read-Alouds).

Being Aware of Street Signs

Introduce or review "Signs" (Community: Poster 3) and make copies of the traffic sign patterns for children to color and cut out. Help children describe a sign's shape and color for others to point to or name the sign. Encourage children to ask family members to help look for each kind of sign in their neighborhood.

Making a Map

Show children some simple maps and then invite them to help make a map on a bulletin board. Model the use of words like *intersection, one-way, two-way, crosswalk, stop sign,* and *traffic light* as children arrange gray strips of paper to lay out streets and discuss where signs might be needed. Copy the sign patterns **(page 000)** for children to color, cut out, and glue in place. Children might draw lines and arrows to designate crosswalks and one-way or two-way streets, and name the streets after themselves, for animals, or after favorite characters from stories or poems.

Have children cut out pictures of people, cars, and other vehicles to move along the map's streets.

Enjoying Related Literature

Share Emily McLeod's *Bear's Bicycle* and introduce or review "Stop, Look, Listen," "City Street," "Traffic Light," "Yes or No," "Alas!" and read and sing "Stop Sign's Song" (all in Related Read-Alouds).

See Meet the Poets, page 187.

Streets

The streets go up,
the streets go down,
and in and out
about the town,

And on the streets
the autos run
two by two
and one by one,

And at each street
I stop to see . . .
for fear the autos
won't see *me*.

Aileen Fisher

"Streets" by Aileen Fisher.
Reprinted by permission of the author.

Animals

Unit 4

1. Goldie

2. Elephant

3. Froggie, froggie

4. Beehive

5. Six Speckled Hens

6. Tiger

7. Polka-Dot Caterpillar

8. Wild Geese

RESPONDING to
Hey, Bug!

by LILIAN MOORE

Introducing the Poem

Children will love hearing you read this poem as if you're talking to a real bug. Place your hand flat and have a pretend bug crawl up and over a finger. Using your hands and arm, make the wall, tower, and bug town. Children enjoy watching the "bug" crawl off to explore a wall, the ceiling, or the underside of a tabletop.

For repeated readings, invite each child to pretend to choose a bug from a "bug bag." Encourage children to say the poem with you to see if their bugs will stay to play.

Using Logic

Use your hands to make each structure and ask children why they couldn't sit on the wall, climb the tower, or live in the bug town. Children like to talk about being too big as they try to fit their feet in the "bug town." Ask why bugs don't stay to play and why another kind of cookie probably wouldn't help.

Asking Helpful Bugs to Stay

Talk about the important jobs that helpful bugs do. Examples might be butterflies that carry pollen from flower to flower to make fruits and seeds, bees that make honey for people to eat, or ladybugs that eat insects that would destroy farmers' crops.

Help children substitute a helpful bug's name in the poem's first line and then talk about the bug's important job. Encourage children to ask family members to help them look for helpful bugs in their neighborhood.

Shooing Pesky Bugs Away

Talk about bothersome bugs, such as flies and mosquitoes that bite, termites that chew on wood, or boll weevils that eat cotton crops. Model an innovation on the poem, such as "Fly, don't stay! Shoo! Go away!" and help children "talk" to other pesky bugs.

Making Buggy Bugs

Use individual egg carton cups, rocks, pebbles, sea shells, or bark chips to make bugs, or mix popcorn and melted caramels to shape edible bugs with raisin eyes.

Exploring Insect Sounds

Share Eric Carle's *The Very Quiet Cricket* and then help children identify sounds that other insects make, such as the buzz of a mosquito, wasp, or bee and the chirp of a cicada. Talk about how some bugs, such as termites, ants, and roaches, are silent. Encourage children to ask family members to listen with them to identify sounds of bugs.

Enjoying Related Literature

Children will enjoy looking for Goldbug in Richard Scarry's *Cars and Trucks and Things That Go*. Substitute bug names in Laura Joffe Numeroff's *If You Give a Mouse a Cookie*, and share B. Freschet's song picture book, *The Ants Go Marching*. Read *The Bug Book and Bug Bottle* by Dr. Hugh Danks, *Bugs!* by Patricia and Fredrick McKissack, *The Grouchy Ladybug* by Eric Carle, and *Bugs* by Nancy Winslow Parker and Joan Richards Wright. Introduce or review "Never hug a ladybug," "Lady Bug," "Clickbeetle," "*from* A Firefly," and "Freckles" (all in Related Read-Alouds).

Activity Page 7: Making Bug Puppets

Reproduce the page for each child to color and cut out the bugs to make finger puppets. Help children say the poem as they make their bug puppets "fly" or "crawl." Children might also use string and clothes hangers to make bug mobiles.

Activity Page 8: Who Lives Here?

Reproduce the page for each child to match a home to its bug. Have children cut out the homes, place each over the bug that would live there, and tape pictures down on both sides. Help children cut each picture on the dotted line to make a "window" and then "knock" on each window and ask, "Who lives here?"

Hey, Bug!

Hey, bug, stay!
Don't run away.
I know a game that we can play.

I'll hold my fingers very still
And you can climb a finger-hill.

No, no.
Don't go.

Here's a wall — a tower, too,
a tiny bug town, just for you.
I've a cookie. You have some.
Take this oatmeal cookie crumb.

Hey, bug, stay!
Hey, bug!
Hey!

Lilian Moore

"Hey Bug!" from I FEEL THE SAME WAY by Lilian Moore. Copyright © 1967 by Lilian Moore. Reprinted by permission of Marian Reiner for the author.

Activity Page 7: Hey, Bug!

Bug Puppets

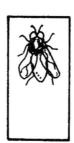

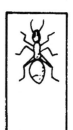

Cut out the finger puppets. Tape one on each finger and make the insects fly or crawl. What might each insect say?

Activity Page 8: Hey, Bug!

Who Lives Where?

Cut out the insects and their homes. Place each home over the picture of the insect that lives there, and tape both sides. Cut through the center of the home and open the "window" to find out who lives where.

RESPONDING To

Goldie

by MARGARET TAPIA

Introducing the Poem

Display the poster and read the poem aloud. Then help children use the illustration to tell which child is getting a fish for a pet and which child wishes for a pet fish. Ask what the fish will be named and why.

Swimming Through a Fishy Tale

Encourage children to dramatize and join in to say "just like fish" as you improvise a story about some children in a school who fooled their teachers into thinking they were really a school of fish. As an analogy between the children and the many sizes, types, and colors of fish, you might weave the children's names and descriptions of their clothing into the story. Tell how the children flapped their arms as if they had fins (just like fish), swam around silently (just like fish), kept their heads straight ahead as if they had no necks (just like fish), opened and closed their mouths (just like fish), and napped with their eyes open as if they had no eyelids (just like fish). You might end the story by telling how, when the teachers grabbed their fishing poles, the children stopped swimming and sat in their chairs as if they feared they'd be caught (just like fish).

Children will enjoy moving like the fish in "Fishy Fishy" and hearing you read "To Catch a Fish" (both in Related Read-Alouds).

Finding Gold or Shiny Things

Help children search the classroom and look in books, magazines, and catalogs to spot gold-colored or shiny items. Children might identify each item by saying, "This (item) shines like gold just like Goldie!"

Invite children to use a commercial polish or salt and white vinegar to shine tarnished copper or gold objects.

Creating a Sea Mural

Share Disney's recording "Under the Sea" from *The Little Mermaid* and Sharon, Lois, and Bram's "Five Little Fishes." Cover a wall area with butcher paper and draw wavy lines near the top to represent the water's surface. Paint the "sea" below the waves and then draw or cut and glue pictures of all kinds of fish and underwater plant life.

Exploring Pet Ownership

If possible, take children to visit a pet shop or animal shelter where they can ask questions about the care required for different kinds of animals. Share "The Goldfish" and "Cat" (both in Related Read-Alouds), Barbara Cohen's *The Carp in the Bathtub*, Pamela Allen's *My Cat Maisie*, Leo Lionni's *Swimmy*, or *Poonam's Pets* by Andrew and Diane Davies.

Help children find pictures to represent the kinds of pets they and their families own. Glue pictures down the left side of chart paper and have children mark tallies or color squares to the right to indicate pet ownership. Count squares or compare the bar lengths to see which pets are most and least popular.

Exploring Pet Wishes

Share "Fish Wish" and "I Had a Little Pig" (both in Related Read-Alouds) and Steven Kellogg's *Can I Keep Him?* Then illustrate the children's pet wishes on a bar graph (see above) or invite children to dictate sentences that tell about pets they'd like to own and why those pets may or may not be good choices for their homes. Encourage children to illustrate their words and then share their wishes and thoughts with family members at home.

Making Fish Puppets

Cut the fish pattern (page 272) on the dotted line and glue one piece to the edge of the top half of a spring-type clothespin and the other piece to the bottom half. Draw an eye on the top half and squeeze the clothespin.

Goldie

I'll name him Goldie,

'cause he shines like gold.

My friend would like to buy him,

but he's already sold!

Margaret Tapia

"Goldie" by Margaret Tapia.
Used by permission of the author.

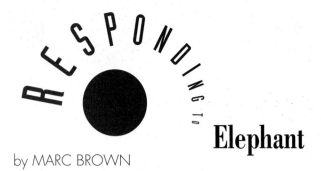

RESPONDING To Elephant

by MARC BROWN

Sharing a Riddle

Before sharing the poster, omit the title and present the poem as a riddle. Ask children to watch your movements and listen to your words to name the animal you're pretending to be. You might place markers on children's right feet and hands before they join you for a second reading. Encourage children to share the riddle at home.

Listening for Information

Invite discussion about the poster's illustration. Then have children listen to the poem to tell the words the elephant uses to describe itself. Track and read the words *gray*, *big*, and *slow* as children respond.

Counting Feet

Invite volunteers to point to the elephant's feet in the illustration as children count in unison. Help children group themselves to see how many children need to stand together in order to have four feet like an elephant.

List other animals that have four feet. Compare a child's one *pair* of feet to two pairs on an elephant or four pairs of tentacles on an octopus.

Making Size Comparisons

Draw and cut out four 9 to 12-inch roundish shapes. Lay out the "elephant's footprints" for children to compare the size to that of their own feet. How many children's right or left feet fit on one "elephant's footprint"?

Finding Where Elephants Live

Help children use a map or globe to find Africa where African elephants live and India where Asiatic or Indian elephants live. Talk about parades, circus events, and zoo exhibits as you discuss why people move elephants from Africa or India to other parts of the world. Point out other countries and help children think about how people move elephants across oceans.

Learning What Elephants Do

Elephants entertain people, but what else do they do? Tell children that elephants in India and other Asian countries help people do heavy work like moving huge logs. Invite children to show how elephants might carry logs in their trunks or on their backs. To illustrate how wild elephants in Africa and India help other animals, have several children pretend to be zebras. Explain that a big, strong elephant clears paths for smaller animals as you move chairs and other things out of your way to lead the "zebras" around the room. Pretend to dig a hole as you tell children that elephants also use their tusks to dig deep holes that fill up with water for smaller animals to drink. Then encourage thought about why elephants need to be protected from hunters.

Greeting a Friend

Explain that elephants greet each other by touching trunks much like people greet each other by shaking hands. Have children use their hands as "trunks" to greet "elephant" friends. Then invite children to be themselves to shake right hands with others. Have children share any special customs their families use when greeting people.

Children might do the "Hokey-Pokey" and then innovate on the text and be elephants who sing about their front and hind feet, trunks, tails, tusks, and ears.

Making Elephants

Make peanut butter dough by mixing two cups of dry milk, two cups of peanut butter, and one cup of honey. Invite children to use the dough to mold elephants or their trunks, tails, feet, tusks, and ears.

Make paper cup puppets by taping paper ear shapes to the sides of foam cups. Draw or paint eyes and mouth and punch a hole for the index finger to serve as a trunk.

Enjoying Related Literature

Introduce "The Graceful Elephant," "Zoo," and "The Elephant" and read "Eletelephony" (all in Related Read-Alouds). Share Raffi's song, "Willoughby Wallaby Woo," and read *The Trouble with Elephants* by Chris Ridell or any of Laurent de Brunhoff's books about Babar.

See Meet the Poets, page 184.

Elephant

Right foot, left foot, see me go.

I am gray and big and slow.

I come walking down the street

With my trunk and four big feet.

Marc Brown

"Elephant" diagrams by Marc Brown from PLAY
RHYMES by Marc Brown. Copyright © 1987 by
Marc Brown. Used by permission of the author.

Froggie, froggie

CHINESE RHYME

Making Predictions

Display the poster and ask children to tell what animal word they think will be in this poem. Confirm children's predictions by pointing out *Froggie* in the title. Cover the *-gie* ending with a sticky tab and read the shorter word. Point out the word *hop* and invite children to hop like frogs. Then track the words as you read the poem aloud.

If any children's names and spellings follow the pattern, you might compare the words *Frog* and *Froggie* to names such as *Kim* and *Kimmie* or *John* and *Johnnie*.

Hopping Like Frogs

Children might hop off a balance beam or other low object into a yarn ring "sea." Since children, like the frog in the poem, will want to hop and hop and hop and never stop, you might recite the poem as if you're speaking to frogs and introduce a few words and ideas about frogs each time. Mention that all your "frogs" must be getting ready to *hibernate* in their *burrows* or *in the mud at the bottom of the pond* now that *winter* is coming (or come out of *hibernation* for *summer*). Touch the *smooth* skin of several "frogs" and announce they are definitely not *toads with rough skin*, or pretend to be a buzzing *insect* avoiding a frog's *sticky tongue*. Ask a few "frogs" how many times they've *shed* their *skins* this year *just like snakes*, check for baby *tadpoles* or *polliwogs*, and end each hopping session by asking some *amphibians* to hop from their *water* and others to hop from their *land* to join you.

Making Frog Puppets

Children can recycle flip-top sandwich or salad-bar containers to make frog puppets. Paint the eyes and mouth or glue felt pieces and buttons in place. Tape two long legs on the bottom, a short leg on either side, and place sticky tape on a red pipe cleaner or accordion-folded paper inside for

the tongue. Cut a hole above the container's hinge to make a child-sized handhold.

In the absence of time or materials, have children place their palms together and rotate hands so that backs of hands face the floor and ceiling. The wrists form a hinge as hands open and close to "snap" at every insect around!

Eating Like Frogs

Invite children to draw or cut out and glue pictures of all sorts of insects on narrow strips of paper. Help children use clothespins to hang the insects from a low clothesline in the room. Some children can have their puppets (see above activity) "catch the flying insects" by pulling them off the clothesline, while others blow or fan the line to make the insects "fly."

At other times, help children count the number of flying insects before and after a "frog" comes by or count how many insects one frog or partner frogs catch.

Help children think about what happens to the frogs in ponds and lakes when people throw trash and garbage in the water. Talk about what happens to the number of insects if frogs are poisoned by pollution and how people's lives are affected if there are too many pesky insects.

Making Frog Sounds

Invite children to make sounds like frogs might make as you write words like "Croak" or "Rib-bit."

Discuss how the vocal cords in the throats of frogs (and people) vibrate to make sound when air is forced out of the lungs. Then help children recycle toilet tissue tubes to make kazoos. Use a rubber band to secure waxed paper over one end of the tube, punch a tiny hole on the side of the tube, and hum through the open end.

Reading More About Frogs

Share Raffi's song, "Five Little Frogs," Arnold Lobel's *Frog and Toad Pop-Up Book* and Marc Brown's *Can You Jump Like a Frog?* Children will enjoy "Hoppity" and "The Frog on the Log" and can add music to sing "Mr. Frog is Full of Hops" and "Glunk, Glunk, Glunk" (all in Related Read-Alouds). Share the song picture book, *The Foolish Frog* by R. Seeger and C. Seeger.

Froggie, froggie

Froggie, froggie,
Hoppity-hop!
When you get to the sea
You do not stop.

Plop!

Chinese Rhyme

Beehive

by ANONYMOUS

Enjoying the Fingerplay

Present the poem as a fingerplay before sharing the poster. Hold up a fist to introduce the "hive" and bring one finger out of the fist at a time. Make fingers "fly" overhead at the end.

Display the poster and help children count the bees in the illustration and then join in as you repeat the fingerplay.

Dramatizing the Poem

Invite five children to be bees who hide in a large box in the room. Help others recite the poem chorally as the "bees" come out of the "hive."

Singing the Poem

Invite children to listen to the recorded song and then sing along while presenting the fingerplay or playing the roles of the bees.

Staging a Puppet Show

Reproduce the bee pattern (page 272) for children to color, cut out, and attach to popsicle sticks, small paper bags, or paper cups. Or use a black marker to draw stripes around yellow balloons and add eyes and yarn handles. Children can take turns having their bee puppets perform as others recite or sing the poem. To adapt the poem so everyone can perform at once for family members and friends, use sticky tabs on the poster to substitute *are* for *is* and add *s* to *beehive* and *hive*.

Being Bees

Share *From Blossom to Honey* by Ali Mitgutsch, *Cycle of a Bee* by Jill Bailey, and *Honeybee* by Barrie Watts. Talk about how honeybees, like people, live together in families. Help children play the roles of bee family members. One girl might be the queen bee who lays eggs but does no other work, while several boys can be drones or male honeybees who do no work except to keep the queen bee company. Several girls can be the worker bees who do all the chores, such as build and guard the hive, care for the baby bees, fly out to collect nectar and pollen from flowers, care for the nectar that becomes honey, and feed and care for the queen. Children might act out how bees become upset and disorganized if the queen bee leaves the hive for a bit.

Making Comparisons

Encourage children to talk with family members to compare the roles of male and female bees in a bee family to those of males and females in a human family.

Share "If the Spider Could Talk" (Related Read-Alouds) and tell children that a bee, like a spider, won't bite unless it is hurt or scared. Help children compare a bee's three pairs of legs to a spider's four pairs and then talk and write about how a bee might feel when a human runs away from it.

Appreciating the Work of Bees

Explain that a honeybee makes honey and is the only insect that produces food for people. Share "Cluck, Cluck, Red Hen" (Related Read-Alouds) and *What's on My Plate?* by Ruth B. Gross. Then help children list some foods animals produce.

Invite children to taste honey and, if possible, feel the smooth and waxy texture of a piece of beeswax which comes from the honeycomb and is used to make candles, gum, glues, and polishes.

Listening for "Bzzzzz"

List more things that make a *bzzzzz* sound, such as an alarm clock, doorbell, or power saw. Have children ask family members to listen for *bzzzzz* sounds with them at home.

Read "Clickbeetle" and "An earthworm doesn't" (both in Related Read-Alouds). Share the recording of "Over in the Meadow" or Ezra Jack Keats' song picture book by the same name.

See Meet the Poets, page 192.

See Adding Music, page 167.

Beehive

Here is the beehive
But where are the bees?
Hiding away
Where nobody sees.
But now they are coming
Out of the hive —
One
    Two
        Three
            Four
                Five
Bzzzzzzzzzzzzzzzz!

Anonymous

"Beehive" Melody by Babs Bell Hajdusiewicz.
Accompaniment by Janet Cubic Sima

Six Speckled Hens

by BABS BELL HAJDUSIEWICZ

Telling a Story

Display the printless poster and tell children the poem's title. Model use of the words *six* and *speckled* as children talk about the hens' preparation for and care of baby chicks. Point out the seedlings and help children use their gradual changes to sunflowers to talk about the passage of time as they tell the hens' story in their own words.

Sharing the Poem

Help children feel the poem's rhythm and repetition as you read aloud. You'll want to accent the rhythm of words in three's as you read the last two lines of each stanza. During repeated readings, divide the group in half to say each repetitive line chorally.

Dramatizing the Poem

Invite three groups of children to be the hens, eggs, and chicks. Children can check for six members in each group by using the illustration to match one child to one hen and so on. Help children think about how to stage the production. For example, each hen might stand in front of or above an egg and each egg might hug a chick to suggest the chick is "inside." Encourage children to recite the poem chorally or recite along with the recording as they act. Present the play for friends and family.

At other times, you might have children face the same directions as the hens and chicks in the poster's illustrations.

Learning about Eggs

Gently tap the shell of a raw egg and discuss how the hard shell protects a baby chick while it's growing inside. Read "Baby Chick" (Related Read-Alouds) and talk about how the chick breaks the shell when it's ready to be hatched. Explain that only eggs that have been fertilized will have chicks in them and that a farmer holds eggs up to a special light to see which ones have chicks inside. Help children think about which eggs go to stores for families to buy and eat.

Comparing Eggs

Invite children to compare the texture and color of brown and white eggs and make predictions about how each will look inside. Crack the eggs onto identical dishes for children to inspect the yolks, whites, and the insides of the shells. Repeat to compare cooked and uncooked eggs or small, medium, large, and extra-large eggs. You may want to draw a comparison here to the different outer appearances of people.

Afterwards, whip and scramble the raw eggs or make eggnog. Use shells in art projects or crush and bury them in a potted plant. Use an egg slicer for hard-boiled egg slices or slice eggs in half, crush yolks with a fork, add salad dressing, and spoon the dip into the halves to make deviled eggs.

Working with Six

Help children place six items in six paper cups or separated egg carton cups as they tell the story of any of the poster's six scenes. Model arranging the cups in two groups of three while chanting the last two lines of any stanza from the poem. Then help children explore other ways to arrange six cups such as 2+2+2, 4+2, 2+4, 5+1, or 1+5. Provide copies of the poem for children to repeat these activities at home.

Enjoying Related Literature

Share "The Rooster" and sing "Cluck, Cluck, Red Hen" (both in Related Read-Alouds) or share Sharon, Lois, and Bram's recording of "Chicken Medley." Children will enjoy listening for rhyming words in Colin and Jacqui Hawkins' *Jen the Hen*, or hearing Steven Kellogg's *Chicken Little* and Margot Zemach's retelling of hen stories in *The Little Red Hen: An Old Story*.

See Meet the Poets, page 189.

Six Speckled Hens

Six speckled hens
build six straw nests.
Busy, Busy, Busy!
Busy, Busy, Busy!

Six speckled hens
lay six brown eggs.
Cluck, Cluck, Cluck!
Cluck, Cluck, Cluck!

Six speckled hens
warm six brown eggs.
Shhh, Shhh, Shhh!
Shhh, Shhh, Shhh!

Six sharp bills
tap six brown eggs.
Peck, Peck, Peck!
Peck, Peck, Peck!

Six baby chicks
break six brown eggs.
Crack, Crack, Crack!
Crack, Crack, Crack!

Six baby chicks
leave six broken shells.
Wobble, Wobble, Wobble!
Wobble, Wobble, Wobble!

Six speckled hens
find six wiggly worms.
Tug, Tug, Tug!
Tug, Tug, Tug!

Six hungry chicks
eat six wiggly worms.
Gobble, Gobble, Gobble!
Gobble, Gobble, Gobble!

Six sleepy chicks
take six quiet naps.
Zzzz, Zzzz, Zzzz!
Zzzz, Zzzz, Zzzz!

Babs Bell Hajdusiewicz

RESPONDING To

Tiger

by MARY ANN HOBERMAN

Enjoying the Poem

Display the poster and discuss the illustration. If possible, use a tiger puppet as you read the animal's warnings slowly to emphasize the word *might* and dramatize the words *Grrr* and *growl*.

Growling and Howling

Children will enjoy imitating the tiger's growl and then pretending to be other growling animals such as lions, bears, or scared or angry dogs. Share "The Lion Roars with a Fearful Sound" (Related Read-Alouds) and Sharon, Lois, and Bram's recording, "Grandpa's Farm."

Focus on rhyming sounds by inviting children to imitate animal sounds and add rhyming words in sentences such as "We are tigers who *growl* and *howl*" or "We are horses who *neigh* for *hay*." Encourage children to initiate serious and silly sentences around ideas such as dogs who *bark* in the *dark* or humans who *walk* and *talk*.

Recognizing "Tiger Stripes"

Build awareness of stripes by pointing out any obvious stripes in children's clothing and your own. Then focus on less obvious striped patterns on clothing such as ribbed cuffs of socks, shirts, or sweaters, bottoms and sides of gym shoes, or woven threads in fabrics. Help children look for striped effects on windows, heating vents, or the ceiling.

At other times, children might identify other striped animals such as skunks, zebras, some kinds of cats and butterflies, or the banded armadillo.

Wearing "Tiger Stripes"

Prepare for a "Tiger Stripes Day" by encouraging children to point out stripes in clothing, wallpapers, wood paneling, fences, and the like to family members at home. Invite everyone to wear striped clothing on the special day and to snack on vegetable sticks arranged in striped patterns or crackers striped with honey, peanut butter, or jelly applied with squeeze bottles.

Creating Stripes of All Kinds

Lined paper can provide guides for children to glue various materials such as spaghetti, paper strips, popsicle sticks, toothpicks, or straws to form striped patterns. Children might also to make flags, weave paper strips into placemats, or make popsicle-stick trivets for use at home.

Identifying Real and Pretend

Compare the real tiger in Helen Cowcher's *Tigress* to the make-believe tigers in Robert Kraus' *Leo the Late Bloomer* and Muriel Blaustein's *Play Ball, Zachary*.

Discuss how the poet has pretended the tiger could talk like a human. Invite children to show how a real tiger seems to say "stay away" as it glares with its eyes, bares its teeth to growl, or fiercely stalks around.

Discuss how animals growl to protect themselves. Encourage children to talk about times they've seen or heard dogs, cats, snakes, or hamsters hiss or growl.

Writing a New Poem

Share "Zoo" (Related Read-Alouds) and then use sticky tabs to model how another word like *lion* might be substituted in the poster poem's title and first line. Help children notice that the word *striped* doesn't make sense for a lion. Reread the first two lines for children to suggest words like *covered, dressed (in)* or *wearing (this)* that could complete the thought and make sense. Help children dictate the new poem as you write it on chart paper. Children might draw or attach a picture to illustrate the poem.

At other times, use the poem's model to present other information such as "I'm a snake shedding my skin" or "I'm a hen warming my eggs."

Tiger

I'm a tiger

Striped with fur

Don't come near

Or I might Grrr

Don't come near

Or I might growl

Don't come near

Or I might

BITE!

Mary Ann Hoberman

"Tiger" reprinted by permission of Gina Maccoby Literary Agency. Copyright © 1959, copyright renewed 1987 by Mary Ann Hoberman.

Polka-Dot Caterpillar

by GAIL BLASSER RILEY

Enjoying a Fingerplay

Display the poster and read the poem's title. Invite children to listen to the poem as you share a fingerplay. A thumb can be a caterpillar that crawls along your arm and "hides" in a fist which represents the chrysalis. Then rotate your wrists so the backs of your hands touch and spread your fingers away from each other like a butterfly's wings.

Learning about Caterpillars

Tell children that a caterpillar has twelve segments, not including the head, and six eyes on each side of its head. Read Eric Carle's *The Very Hungry Caterpillar* and explain that a caterpillar is a big eater that sheds its skin several times as its grows.

Exploring the Life Cycle of a Butterfly

Talk about how a caterpillar (larva) hatches from a butterfly's egg and begins to eat leaves and fruit. It forms a chrysalis (pupa) around itself and emerges as a full-grown butterfly. (The chrysalis is the pupal stage of most butterflies, though Parnassian butterflies and moths emerge from cocoons.)

Invite children to curl up as if they're inside butterfly eggs, crawl out and pretend to eat and grow, crawl into paper bags (chrysalises), and then emerge with arms extended as "butterflies." Talk about how butterflies carry pollen from flower to flower so fruits and seeds can develop.

Exploring Designs

Explain that a caterpillar and the butterfly it becomes have similar designs. Reproduce the butterfly pattern (page 272) and help children draw caterpillars on their papers. Use sticky dots or crayons to make polka dots on both stages of Monarch or Bronze Copper butterflies.

Encourage children to ask family members to help them look for butterflies and caterpillars and predict the design of each in its previous or later stage.

"Painting" a Butterfly

Place a dab of paint in the middle of a sheet of paper, fold the paper in half, and rub over the paper. The resulting picture should resemble symmetrical butterfly wings.

Making a Giant Caterpillar

Have each of twelve groups contribute one of the caterpillar's segments as another group makes its head. Children can stuff paper bags with newspapers, tape the filled bags together, and paint polka dots or other designs on the segments.

"Planting" a Hairy Caterpillar

To make a caterpillar that resembles the larval stage of the Mourning Cloak or Comma Anglewing butterfly, cut an egg carton in half lengthwise and staple the two rows of cups end to end. Add a paper face and pipe cleaners for antennae. Place soil in each egg cup, sprinkle grass seed over the soil, and add water as needed.

Making More Caterpillars

Glue twelve cotton balls, ping pong balls, small pine cones, yarn pom poms, or walnut shells in a row on cardboard backing. Recycled fast food or gum wrappers also work well when wadded in balls. Add a paper face and pipe cleaners for antennae.

Use marshmallow cream or peanut butter as "glue" to join large marshmallows, add raisin eyes and licorice antennae.

Reading Related Literature

Read Denise Fleming's *In the Tall, Tall Grass* and *Dots, Spots, Speckles, and Stripes* by Tana Hoban. Share "Away floats the butterfly," "Little Silk Worms," "The Pretty Butterfly," "The Worried Caterpillar," and "Freckles" (all in Related Read-Alouds).

Polka-Dot Caterpillar

Polka-dot caterpillar,
Wiggle, wiggle, crawl!
Polka Dot! Polka Dot!
Oops! Don't fall!

Polka-dot caterpillar,
Hide, hide, hide!
Polka Dot? Polka Dot?
What's inside?

Gail Blasser Riley

"Polka-Dot Caterpillar" by Gail Blasser Riley.
Reprinted by permission of the author.

97

Wild Geese

JAPANESE RHYME

Introducing the Poem
Display the poster. Talk about how wild geese fly away, unlike those that live in zoos or on farms. Ask children to listen for a word that describes the size of the goose that leads the way .

Dramatizing the Poem
Label the north, south, east, and west sides of the room. Discuss the directions and encourage children to "fly" to the south end of the room as you talk about how geese migrate south in the wintertime. Mention that geese have oil glands in their tails and can rub oil over their feathers to waterproof themselves. Share "Drippy Weather" (Related Read-Alouds), "The north wind doth blow" (Nursery Rhymes: Poster 7), and Raffi's recording, "Six Little Ducks."

Singing the Poem
Sing the poem's words as a two-part round or invite children to sing along with the recording as one child pretends to be the big goose by holding a large playground ball and leading the way for others who hold smaller balls.

Discussing Flying
Help children name more flying animals. Share "If Only I Could Fly" (Related Read-Alouds) and talk about how people fly. You may want to discuss the make-believe flying powers of superheroes and read *Tuesday*, David Wiesner's fantasy about flying frogs.

Being Geese and Goslings
Read *Are You My Mother?* by P. D. Eastman. Make an equal number of word cards that say "goose" or "gosling" and give one to each child. Each gosling might say, "I am a little gosling looking for my parent. Are you a goose?" Others might respond with "No, I am a gosling" or "Yes, I am a goose." Continue until each gosling is paired with a goose. Repeat the activity for pigs and piglets, sheep and lambs, and so on, or include a mixture of animals.

Enjoying a Related Poem
Talk about how geese fly in patterns, and share "Feathered Letters" (Related Read-Alouds). Duplicate the goose pattern (page 272) for each child to color and then glue magnetic tape on the back. Invite children to place geese in the shape of a V, Z, or Y on a magnetic board and then take their magnets home to use on the refrigerator.

Looking at Downy Feathers
Use words such as *soft, down, light, feathery,* and *fluffy* as children examine feathers from an old pillow and then use the feathers in art projects.

Telling Who's Where
Share Tana Hoban's *All about Where.* Help children form a line and tell who is *in front of* or *behind* them. Have children turn around to repeat the activity or stand side-to-side to tell who is on their left and right.

Meeting Groups of Animals
Introduce words that name animal groups, such as a *flock, herd, pride, school.* Share Robert McClosky's *Make Way for Ducklings* and Leo Lionni's *Swimmy.*

Flocking Together
Invite children to fringe paper strips in varying lengths and colors to make "feathers." Share the saying, "Birds of a feather flock together," and have children carry their feathers and follow directions, such as "Red feathers, fly to the east side of the room" or "Little feathers tuck your heads under your wings."

Flying Bag Kites
Invite children to hold the handles of a shopping bag behind them and run into the wind, or tie string to the handles to see how a bag kite can "peacefully fly away" on a windy day. Encourage children to invite family members to fly bag kites with them at home.

See Adding Music, page 182.

Wild Geese

Wild geese,
wild geese,
fly away!
Big goose ahead
as you lead the way;
Small geese behind
as you fly away.
Peacefully,
peacefully
fly away!

Kari,
kari,
watare!
Okina kariwa sakini;
Chisana kariwa atoni.
Nakayoku watare!

Japanese Rhyme

Nature

Unit 5

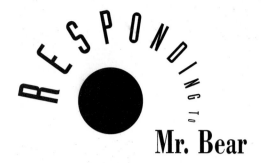

Mr. Bear

by BABS BELL HAJDUSIEWICZ

Enjoying the Narrative

Children will enjoy hearing you read the poem dramatically as if you're telling a story that happened to you. Show an air of self-confidence in controlling a bear, use your hand to demonstrate "halt," point your finger for each "Mr. Bear!" and strike a charming pose for *debonair*.

For repeated readings, encourage children to supply the rhyming words at the ends of lines and join in to say each "Mr. Bear!" At other times, play on the poem's language to give poetic reminders, such as "Mr. James, Mr. James, now don't you dare take all of these blocks, leaving none to share" or "Dorie Ann, Dorie Ann, now don't you dare go out of this room without tucking your chair."

Dramatizing the Poem

Children can take turns being Mr. Bear or the narrator as others use their bodies to form the cave and chair. Or use props such as a stuffed bear, some clothes, a pillow for a chair, and a cardboard box children decorate as a cave. Help children use their own words as they dramatize the story.

Identifying Real and Pretend

Help children recognize that some bears hibernate in caves for protection from cold and snow and that bears growl to protect themselves. Discuss why a person could not control a bear in a cave, and talk about the fantasy of dressing a bear in clothes.

Dressing Stuffed Animals

Provide clothes or help children use paper bags and newspapers to make clothes to dress stuffed animals they bring from home. Help children innovate on the poem's text to include the animals' names and other words that apply.

Sorting Clothes for Mr. Bear

Help children use magazines and catalogs to find pictures of hats, clothing, and shoes and boots to display under headings such as "Headwear," "Bodywear," and "Footwear." Or add a stuffed bear dressed in underwear and title the display "Mr. Bear, Don't Go Out In Your Underwear!"

Growling at Rhyming Words

Reread the poem or play the recording and ask children to growl like Mr. Bear might each time they hear a word that rhymes with his name.

Preparing Mr. Bear Treats

Use a cookie cutter to cut bear shapes from bread slices. Invite children to use peanut butter or jelly and raisins to "dress" Mr. Bear in polka-dotted underwear or other clothing.

Enjoying Related Literature

Read Judith Barrett's books, *Animals Should Definitely Not Wear Clothing* and *Animals Should Definitely Not Act Like People,* Eve B. Feldman's *Animals Don't Wear Pajamas*, and Nancy White Carlstrom's *Jesse Bear, What Will You Wear?* Share "Shopping Day" (Community: Poster 5), "Grizzly Bear" (Related Read-Alouds), and bear poems in *Bear in Mind* by Bobbye S. Goldstein.

Activity Page 9: Dressing Mr. Bear

Reproduce the page and have children tell about the pictures and cut them out. Children can stack the pictures in order to show how Mr. Bear might get dressed and then staple the pictures together at the top, or arrange them in order to make a book or frieze that tells Mr. Bear's story.

Activity Page 10: Mr. Bear's Closet

Reproduce the page for each child. Have children cut out the pictures of clothing items and glue each where it belongs in Mr. Bear's closet. Children might "fold the underwear" before "putting it away."

See Meet the Poets, page 189.

Mr. Bear

I'll tell you a story of how old Mr. Bear
Almost went out in his underwear!
Mr. Bear was asleep when he had a bad dream
And woke himself up with a monstrous SCR-E-E-E-A-M!
He was heading outside of his comfortable cave
When I stopped him abruptly to make him behave.

And I said:
"Mr. Bear! Mr. Bear! Now don't you dare
Go out of this cave in your underwear!
Mr. Bear! Mr. Bear! You must be aware
It's winter outside; there's snow in the air!"
He growled at me as if to say,
"Get out of here! Get out of my way!"

But I said:
"Mr. Bear! Mr. Bear! I know it's unfair
To be rudely awakened in a scary nightmare.
But Mr. Bear! Mr. Bear! Please stay right there!
Don't leave your cave! There's snow everywhere!"
He looked at me with eyes half-closed;
Then G-R-O-W-L-E-D again! I nearly froze!

But I said:
"Mr. Bear! Mr. Bear! You'll have to prepare!
A bear mustn't go out in just underwear!
Mr. Bear! Mr. Bear! Sit down in your chair!
If you want to go out, you'll need something to wear!
Let's see, Mr. Bear, here's a coat and a pair
Of boots and hat. . .mmmm, you'll look debonair!
Mr. Bear? Mr. Bear? Well, I do declare!
Mr. Bear is snoring in his underwear!"

Babs Bell Hajdusiewicz

Activity Page 9: Mr. Bear

Dressing Mr. Bear

Cut out the pictures to show how Mr. Bear should dress for winter. Stack the pictures in order and staple them at the top. Flip the pages as you tell Mr. Bear's story.

Mr. Bear's Closet

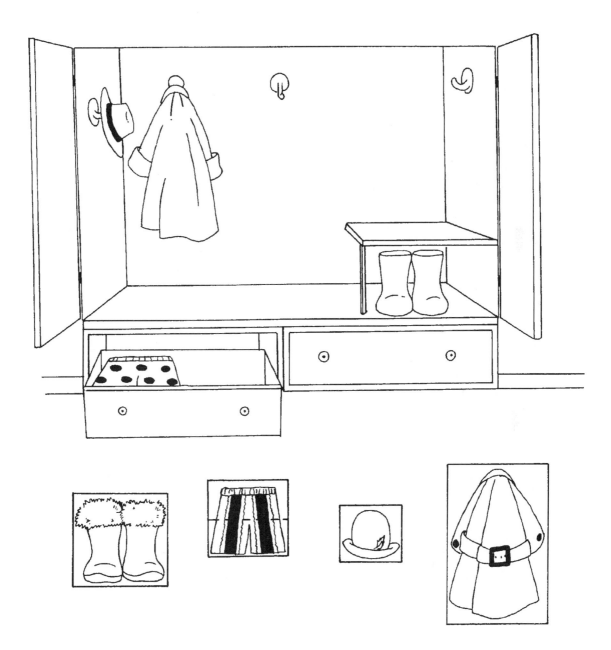

Cut out the pictures of Mr. Bear's clothes. Help Mr. Bear put them away neatly in his closet.

from **Wind**

translated by SYLVIA CASSEDY

Setting the Stage

Make a point of modeling the use of words like *mystery, mysterious, solve,* and *solution* when children need to find something that's missing, hear unfamiliar noises, or experience other puzzling situations.

Solving a Mystery

Display the poster and ask children to look at the illustration and listen to the poem to see if they can solve a mystery. You might offer an extra clue by "stretching" the word *who* in each line to sound like wind. Help children give reasons for their thoughts.

Sounding Like the Wind

Children will enjoy saying the word *who* to sound like wind. Tell children you'll write the word just the way they say it as you write "Who-o-o-o-o." Children will be fascinated to see you add more *o*'s as their "wind" blows on and on and on!

Sensing the Wind

Tell children that wind is air that moves across the earth where we live. Talk about how the wind is invisible but we can see how it moves things, we can feel it, and sometimes we can hear it. Have children wave their hands rapidly to feel the windy air. Share *Feel the Wind* by Arthur Dorros and "Who Has Seen the Wind?" (Related Read Alouds). Children might sing the latter poem's words while on a walk to feel the wind, listen for its sound, and watch it move the grass or flags or leaves.

Learning about Mangoes

If a mango is an unfamiliar fruit, share pictures from an encyclopedia and tell children about this spicy yellow, red, or green fruit that grows on a mango tree. Ask children to use their hands to show an apple's size. Explain that mangoes are about that size. Using a map or globe, point out southeastern Asia where mangoes first grew. Tell children that people in other hot, wet places also grow and eat mangoes.

Finding India on a Map

Point out India on a map or globe and tell children that this poem was first written in one of the languages spoken by many people in India. Explain that Sylvia Cassedy knows that language and English, too, so she rewrote the poem in English.

Using Wind to Move Things

Children can experience how wind moves things when they fly kites, make and use paper fans, streamers, or pinwheels, blow on water in a shallow pan, blow through straws to move poster paint around to make designs on paper, or blow to make paper or other light objects move across a table. Children might have a water race by blowing on boats or rafts made from foam packaging.

Seeing How Print Works

Ask children to name a fruit that might be blown off a tree in their neighborhood. Using a sticky tab on the poster, show how that fruit's name can replace *mango*. Reread the poem and help children decide whether *yellow* is the right color word to describe the new fruit. Repeat for other suggested fruits.

Publishing a Mystery

Share "Who-o-o-o-o Am I?" (Related Read-Alouds) and invite children to publish a mystery book. Right-hand pages could read *Who-o-o-o-o am I?* with left-hand pages containing the rest of each question along with drawings or pictures from magazines. The last two lines might go on the back cover. Invite illustrators to sign the book before making copies for sharing with family members at home.

Enjoying Related Literature

Share Patricia C. McKissack's *Mirandy and Brother Wind,* Julia Hoban's *Amy Loves the Wind, The Wind Blew* by Pat Hutchins, or "Wouldn't You?" (Related Read-Alouds).

from **Wind**

Who shook the yellow mango?
Who dropped it from its tree?
Who rattled all the branches?
Who tried to hide from me?

translated by Sylvia Cassedy

"Wind" (original title "Who?") from MOON-UNCLE, MOON-
UNCLE: RHYMES FROM INDIA by Sylvia Cassedy and Parvathi
Thampi. Reprinted by permission of Ellen Cassedy.

RESPONDING To Rainbow Colors

by BABS BELL HAJDUSIEWICZ

Introducing the Poem
Display the poster and read the poem's title. Talk about the rainbow in the illustration and ask what the child is painting. Help children identify each color of the rainbow as you read its word in the poem.

Counting the Colors
Reread the poem for children to listen for a number that tells how many colors are in a rainbow. List the numerals 1 through 7 on chart paper and write one of the rainbow's color words (red, orange, yellow, green, blue, indigo, and violet) next to each. Help children match crayons to the rainbow's colors and then count seven crayons or match color words on crayons to the same words on the chart or poster. You might tell children that we usually see only four or five colors on a real rainbow because the colors blend together.

Singing the Words
Using the tune, "Twinkle, Twinkle, Little Star," sing the poem's words, and repeat the first stanza.

Talking about Rainbows
Help children identify rain and sun as necessary elements to have a rainbow. Tell children that people in North Africa say a rainbow is like a "bride of the rain." Explain that just like a bride and groom go together in a wedding, a rainbow goes with rain because there has to be rain to have a rainbow. Help children think about why Vietnamese people might say a rainbow is like a "little window in the sky."

Making Rainbow Arcs
Tie chalk to one end of heavy string. Have one child hold the loose end as another child stretches the chalk end to draw an arc on a sidewalk or pavement. Shorten the string at intervals and help others draw more arcs for seven "ribbons" in all. Play the recording of the song to assist children as they use chalk to color the "ribbons" red to violet from outside to inside.

Children might draw rainbows on paper taped to the table or floor and then share the poem and rainbow with family members.

Observing "Rainbows"
Leave a jar of water out overnight. Help children observe the shapes and patterns that diffuse through the water when one drop each of red, yellow, and blue food coloring is added. Budding scientists might repeat the experiment with hot water or sugar water or drop the colors from varied heights.

At another time, pour a thin layer of cooking oil into a jar of water. Watch drops of food coloring move through the oil, make circles in the water, and settle to the bottom.

Making "Scratch & See" Rainbows
You might play Heather Bishop's recording of "Somewhere Over the Rainbow" during this activity. Have children rub hard to cover paper with different crayon colors and then use black crayon to color over the colors. Provide toothpicks or pencil points for scratching through the black layer to see the rainbow of colors beneath.

Experimenting with Color
Provide clear plastic cups, water, and food coloring for children to explore the effects when one, two, or more drops of red, yellow, or blue food coloring are added to clear water. Children might create shades of each color, name the colors, and then arrange them in order from lightest to darkest.

At another time, mix the primary colors to create secondary colors, green, orange, and purple. Share Leo Lionni's *Little Blue and Little Yellow*, Arnold Lobel's *The Great Blueness*, Fulvio Testa's *If You Take a Paint Brush*, or Tana Hoban's books, *Of Colors and Things* and *Is It Red? Is It Blue?*

See Meet the Poets, page 189.

Rainbow Colors

Red, orange, yellow
Green and blue
Indigo
And violet, too!

Bride of the rain
Little window in the sky
An arc of seven colors
When the sun is nearby!

Babs Bell Hajdusiewicz

RESPONDING To **Seeds**

by DELIA FIRA

Exploring Prior Knowledge

Present several foods and have children predict which ones will have seeds inside them. Help children make labels such as "Seeds" and "No Seeds" and then listen to each other's ideas before deciding how to group the foods. Slice or break open the foods for children to observe and then regroup them, if necessary.

Exploring Seeds

Provide a nut cracker and plastic knives for children to help slice and crack many kinds of fruits, vegetables, and nuts such as walnuts, filberts, or pecans. (Note that peanuts and almonds are not true seeds.) Children can scoop out the seeds, compare them for size, color, and texture, and match seeds to their sources to identify what would grow if they were planted. Help children observe that big plants or fruit can grow from tiny *or* large seeds. Children can dry, bake, and eat some seeds, plant some, use some in craft projects, put some out for the birds, and then snack on the nuts, vegetables, and fruits.

Introducing the Poem

For the first reading, lay out an assortment of seeds and recite the poem as if you're simply commenting on what you see. What a natural way to lead into identifying, sorting, and classifying those seeds!

Crafting with Seeds

Help children glue seeds on large letters that spell their names, make noisy shakers from recycled cans and pie tins, glue seeds on string or yarn to make jewelry, make seed collages, or glue seeds in vertical rows for flower stems that sport leaves or flowers.

Exploring How Seeds Travel

To explore how wind, water, people and animals help seeds travel, invite children to blow or fan seeds, pour water over a pile of seeds on a tray, or pick up seeds and walk around as a person or animal might. You might also place old socks over children's shoes and go for a walk in a grassy area. Then carefully remove the socks and collect and sort the seeds that have traveled inside!

Role-Playing Seeds

Place a blanket over a child who role-plays a "seed" that grows slowly as one foot pops out, then a leg, and so on. Read "I Am Growing!" (Related Read-Alouds) for children to think about what growing plants might say if they could talk. Encourage children to play-act being seeds at home.

Making Pine Cone Trees

Dip a pine cone in water and then in potting soil. Sprinkle grass seeds on the moist pine cone and stand it on clay in a clear jar. Close tightly, poke air holes in the lid, and watch a tree begin to grow in a few days.

Sorting and Counting Seeds

Use seeds or beans with obvious variations in size, color, and shape. Tape one of each kind to the front of a small container and provide a mixture of the same seeds or beans for children to sort. Recite the poem's words while children are working!

At another time, have children match the number and kind of seeds in the containers, or color squares on a bar graph to represent seeds or beans that match the samples taped down the left side.

Reading about Growing Things

Share *A Seed, a Flower, a Minute, an Hour* by Joan W. Blos and *Seeds and More Seeds* by Millicent Selsam. Share "I Dig, Dig, Dig," "Little Seeds We Sow in Spring," "Maytime Magic," "My Nipa Hut," "Bird Gardens," or "Tommy" (all in Related Read-Alouds).

Using the Poem's Pattern

Children will enjoy hearing you play on the poem's pattern at various times. Substitute *coats* or *shoes* for *seeds* when children's things are in a pile, or comment on all those *crayons* or *buttons* when children do sorting activities.

See Meet the Poets, 186.

Seeds

So many, many kinds of seeds—
Big seeds
Little seeds
Long seeds
Short seeds
Fat seeds
Thin seeds
Even striped
and speckled seeds
What will grow from all these seeds?
Some flowers, trees, and fruits—
or weeds?

Delia Fira

"Seeds" © 1991 by Delia Fira.
Used by permission of the author

RESPONDING to Copycat

by BABS BELL HAJDUSIEWICZ

Previewing Vocabulary

Explain that a copycat does exactly what someone else does. Then invite children to be copycats who copy your movements *and* your words. Blink and say, "I can blink my eyes." Repeat for other words as needed. To illustrate *trick,* bend over while saying, "I can stand up very tall. . .Uh, oh! That was a *trick*!" Allow volunteers to lead the group.

"Copycats" enjoy singing and acting out "The Hokey-Pokey."

Introducing the Poem

Display the poster and have children listen as you read aloud to see who is a copycat. Ask children how they think the child in the illustration feels about the shadow and why.

Learning about Shadows

Provide opaque and transparent shapes cut from materials such as colored paper, waxed paper, clear and colored plastic, or netting. Have children try to see light through each to predict which materials will make shadows. Children can check their predictions by laying the shapes on an overhead projector. Which materials make shadows on a screen or wall?

Read "Sun Fun" (Related Read-Alouds) and share *Shadow Magic* by Seymour Simon or Tana Hoban's *Shadows and Reflections.*

Playing with Shadows

Children will enjoy making shadow puppets with their fingers on an overhead projector, tracing around shadows on paper or a sidewalk, being copycats as they try to become their partners' shadows, playing Shadow Tag in which "It" tries to tag others' shadows, posing for silhouettes, or going on a shadow hunt. Play Safe Shadows to help children view shade as merely the shadow of a tree, telephone pole, or other object. "Safe" players are on shadows (in the shade) when "It" says, "Stop!"

Being Statues

Take a walk in a park or other area where children can view a statue, or share replicas or pictures of statues through books, brochures, and encyclopedias. Invite children to move to music and "freeze" as statues when the music stops.

Exercising with the Poem

Take children outside on a sunny day or provide a strong light source so that children see their shadows. Read or recite the poem's first stanza as children (and their shadows) do jumping jacks. Then add stanzas by changing the third line to "I stretch to make some airplane wings," "I curl up in a somersault," "I touch my nose and then my toes," and the like. The poem's last stanza invites children (and their "sweaty" shadows) to "cool down" as statues.

Making Copycat "Sandwiches"

Help children staple copycat "sandwiches," carbon paper between two sheets of paper. Allow children to discover what happens when they write on the top sheet or turn the "sandwich" over and write on the backside.

Have children use carbon paper or a copy machine to give copies of special artwork pieces to several family members.

Making Shadow Shapes

Help children discover how the sun bleaches out color and copies an object. Place flat objects on blue or purple paper and set in direct sun for an hour or so. Have children match objects to their "shadows."

Enjoying More Related Poems

Children will enjoy thinking of a shadow as a giant in "Giant," hearing what a shadow might say in "You" and "Your Shadow Says," or chanting and singing "Shadow Me" (all in Related Read-Alouds).

See Meet the Poets, page 189.

Copycat

My shadow is a copycat!
It copies what I do.
I do a bouncy jumping jack,
And Shadow does one, too!

But watch me trick that copycat!
When I stand still and blink,
My shadow is a statue who
Has never learned to wink!

Babs Bell Hajdusiewicz

"Copycat" © 1992 by Babs Bell Hadjdusiewicz.
Reprinted by permission of the author.

RESPONDING To
The Berry Family

by BONNIE KINNE

Assessing Prior Knowledge
Ask who has tasted a blueberry or strawberry. What color is each berry? Which of the two berries is larger? Have children name and describe other berries they've seen or tasted.

Building on Prior Knowledge
Talk about berries as small fruits that grow singly or in a *bunch* on bushes or vines in a berry *patch*. You might tell children about a personal experience of growing, picking, or selecting berries in a store or fruit market.

Use seed catalogs or packages to prepare flannelboard pictures of the berries named in the poem. Help children describe each berry and tell its color. You may want to write each berry's name beside its picture.

Enjoying the Poem
Tell children the poem's title and ask "who" might be in the berry family. Display the poster and help children identify each berry. Children will enjoy your puzzled expression and playful tone of voice in the poem's last lines.

Finding What Doesn't Belong
Talk about what doesn't really belong with all the berries. Play with the sounds and meanings of *bear-y* and *berry*. Help children collect items such as crayons or blocks and include one odd item. Can others identify the odd item and tell why it doesn't belong? You may want to share any of Martin Handford's books about Waldo.

Sensing Berries
If possible, provide several kinds of fresh, canned, or frozen berries or berry products such as jellies, jams, juices, or fruit pops for children to smell and taste. Children will enjoy learning to identify berries by texture, flavor, or fragrance and sensing berry fragrances in products such as gelatins, candies, air fresheners, stickers, or cereals. Encourage children to use their senses to identify berry products at home and during shopping trips with family members.

Adding More Berries
Introduce and add to the poem more kinds of berries such as raspberries, boysenberries, chinaberries, huckleberries, or loganberries.

Meeting the Beary Bunch
Use the list pattern of the poem to talk and write about the seven species of bears including the polar bear, Asiatic black bear, American black bear, big brown bear, sun bear, spectacled bear, and sloth bear. A teddy bear could also be the surprise in a new list poem titled "The Bear Family."

At other times, help children similarly list members of more kinds of families such as apples, cats, contents of a particular room, colors, or children's family members at home. This is a good time to share "The Family of the Sun," "Night Bear," or "My Teddy," or enjoy the sounds and rhythm in "Clickbeetle" (all in Related Read-Alouds).

Being Berry Safe
Tell or remind children that the berries mentioned in the poem are safe to eat but that some berries such as yew berries and mistletoe berries are poisonous and must never be eaten. Encourage children to ask adult family members about any poisonous berries around their homes or in their neighborhood.

Staging the Poem
To prepare for a group presentation, show children how you rewrite the poem to change the *y* in each berry word to *i* plus *es*. Children will enjoy painting paper bag costumes to be the various berries or the teddy bear. As a narrator surveys the different bunches of berries, children might rise from "the patch."

Enjoying Related Literature
Share Bruce Degen's word fun with bears and berries in *Jamberry* or read and sing *Teddy Bears' Picnic* by Jimmy Kenney.

The Berry Family

In the berry patch-
    Blueberry
    Blackberry
    Strawberry
    Gooseberry
    Cranberry
    Elderberry
    Teaberry
    Teddybeary
Teddybeary!
What are YOU doing
In the berry bunch?

Bonnie Kinne

"The Berry Family" by Bonnie Kinne.
Used by permission of the author.

Boom! Bang!

by ANONYMOUS

Assessing Prior Knowledge
Say, "Boom! Bang! Boom! Bang!" and ask what might make those sounds. Encourage dramatization of ideas such as weather, something falling, drums or cymbals, construction noises, or a monster. Then help children decide which of their ideas best fits the poem's title and illustration.

Making Stormy Sounds
Children can accompany the poem's words with rhythm instruments or dramatize each line as follows: bang a metal lid, beat a drum or stomp feet in unison, slice hands through the air, clap hands together, make whistle-like sounds and move side to side, place hands on cheeks in an expression of joy at the end.

Playing with Rhyming Sounds
Accent rhythm as you chant, "Rumpety" several times. Repeat for "Lumpety" and then compare the words' beginning and ending sounds. Invite half the group to chant "Rumpety..." as others follow to chant "Lumpety...." Repeat for *rustles* and *bustles* or other rhyming pairs such as *zooming/booming, clackety/rackety* or *zingy/ringy*.

Enjoy more *onomatopoeia,* or words that imitate sounds, in "Ears Hear" and "POP! POPPITY! POP!" (both in Related Read-Alouds), or share "Marvelous Toy," a song from Lisa Atkinson's *I Wanna Tickle the Fish.*

Eyeing a Storm
Focus on colors and descriptive words such as *light, dark, foggy,* or *stormy* as children cut or tear colored paper to make raindrops, fallen branches, lightning "zig-zags," or clouds for a "Boom! Bang!" collage.

Share James Tisot's print, "A Passing Storm" and discuss colors the artist used to show the storm outside.

Experiencing Static Electricity
Tell children that lightning is a flash of light caused by electricity in the air. Provide balloons and hair combs for children to explore static electricity. Rub a balloon on clothing and watch it stick to a wall or make hair stand up! Briskly comb hair on a dry day and hear the crackle sounds or watch the charged comb pick up bits of paper. Talk about the shock of static electricity when touching metal after shuffling across a carpet. This is a good time to discuss safety around electricity.

Building Vocabulary
Talk about hailstorms, tornadoes, sandstorms, hurricanes, or snowstorms. Invite children to mimic sounds and movements of each and name colors that might be seen. For example, a whisper, moving on tiptoe, and *white* could suggest a snowstorm.

Comparing Feelings
Discuss how the poet seems to like thunderstorms. Then help children share and record their feelings about thunder by inviting each child to color a square on graph paper beside a smily or sad face. Compare lengths of the two lines to see if more children like or dislike thunder. Repeat to compare feelings about lightning. Charlotte Zolotow's *Hold My Hand* and Julia Hoban's *Amy Loves the Rain* illustrate a contrast of feelings about storms, while "Bed Mate" and "April" (both in Related Read-Alouds) focus on more feelings about weather.

Traveling as Light or Sound
Since light travels faster than sound, lightning seems to occur before thunder, but they actually happen at the same time. Have children join hands in two lines to act the parts of lightning and thunder. At a signal, lightning runs, perhaps in a zig-zag pattern, across a gym or outdoor area while thunder stomps at a slow pace. Repeat to reverse roles.

See Meet the Poets, page 192.

Boom! Bang!

Boom, bang, boom, bang!
Rumpety, lumpety, bump!
Zoom, zam, zoom, zam!
Clippety, clappety, clump!
Rustles and bustles
   and swishes and zings —
What wonderful noises
   a thunderstorm brings!

Anonymous

Squirmy Earthworm

by BABS BELL HAJDUSIEWICZ

Dramatizing the Poem

Display the poster and read the poem's title. Talk about how birds search for worms and insects as food for themselves and their babies. Pretend to be the earthworm as you read the poem. Invite children to be earthworms for a second reading and then designate groups as earthworms, raindrops, and blackbirds for repeated readings.

Enjoying a Finger Rhyme

The thumb can be Squirmy who lives in the fist-hole of the same hand. As Squirmy wiggles backwards out of her hole, the other hand can mimic raindrops falling. Squirmy might squirm around the fist-hole and then wiggle inside when the fingers of the other hand become blackbirds. Share "Bunny" (Related Read-Alouds) for another finger rhyme about an animal who lives in a hole.

Singing a Squirmy Song

Sing the poem's words to the tune of "Eensy Weensy Spider."

Watching Earthworms Work

Help children place damp soil and a bit of lettuce in a tall, thin, glass jar to make a home for earthworms. After a rainfall, children can go on an earthworm search on the playground. Place worms in the jar, punch holes in a cover, and tape dark paper around the jar. Observe the earthworms' tunnel work the next day and then help children find a safe spot outside to release the worms. Share Demi's poem, "Little silk worms" (Related Read-Alouds) and her book, *Where is Willie Worm?*

Charting How Animals Move

Help children recognize that earthworms do not run, jump, or hop because they have no feet. Have children draw or glue pictures on a chart to show animals that squirm, hop, fly, or swim to move about.

Identifying Above and Below

Read "An earthworm doesn't" (Related Read-Alouds) and Mary Ann Hoberman's book, *A House Is a House for Me.* Help children list names of some animals that live above and below the ground.

Help children cut out pictures of the listed animals and place each above or below the ground as depicted on a large mural. At another time, depict animals that fly above the earth or swim below the water.

Squirming to the Music

Invite children to wiggle and squirm like earthworms as you play the recorded song. Each time the music stops, "worms" might "freeze" as if they've spotted birds in the area! Share Jon Blake's *Wriggly Pig* about a character who is unable to stop wiggling.

Recognizing Rhyming Sounds

Have children wiggle when they hear words that rhyme with *worm* or *hound* as you say, "Squirmy Worm got a perm" or "The hound ran around on the ground." Then help children make up sentences full of rhyming words or use rhymes to name animals such as Bleep the Sheep, Wiggly Piggly, or Boxy Foxy.

Making Squirmy Worms

Show children how to make worms by rolling clay or by wrapping pipe cleaners around pencils and removing the pencils. Glue a tiny piece of magnetic tape (available at hardware stores) under each worm. Children can move magnets under paper to race their worms across the top. The worms can then go home to hold notes on refrigerator doors.

Creating a New Poem

Substitute names of other kinds of birds in the poem or try having Slithery Snake or Bunny Rabbit be the main character.

See Meet the Poets, page 189.

Squirmy Earthworm

 Squirmy, Squirmy Earthworm
Lives down in the ground.

 But watch her wiggle out
When rain falls all around!

 Squirmy, Squirmy Earthworm
Squirms along the ground.

 But watch her disappear when
Blackbirds come around!

Babs Bell Hajdusiewicz

"Squirmy Earthworm" © 1990 by Babs Bell Hajdusiewicz.
Used by permission of the author.

RESPONDING To

It fell in the city

by EVE MERRIAM

Making Predictions

Display the printless poster and tell children the poem's title. Have them look for shapes of familiar objects in the illustration and tell what they think fell in the city. Encourage children to check their predictions as they listen and join in on the repeated line, "All turned white."

Listening for Color Words

Help children identify a crayon or color chip for each color word they hear as you reread the poem or play the recording.

Another time, have children use appropriately colored blocks or toys to build a city scene. As you read, children can use cotton balls, pillow stuffing, or confetti to make the objects "turn white."

Giving Meaning to Print

Reread the poem for children to notice the absence of the word *snow*. Write "It fell in the city" on chart paper and help children realize that the word *it* refers to snow. Using a sticky tab, model substituting *Snow* for *It*.

Observing Details

Take children for a walk to look for black rooftops, red fire hydrants, and so on. Children should notice that these objects may appear in other colors, too. Interested children may want to make color word substitutions on copies of the poem.

Being "Color Detectives"

Invite children to explore the classroom to find examples of the colors mentioned in the poem. Review the colors by displaying an assortment of one-inch paper squares. Children can make a graph of seven colored rows by adding a paper square of the appropriate color for each "sighting." Compare row lengths or count the squares to tell which color appears most or least often.

Making "Snow"

Use an electric mixer or whip two cups of soap flakes and two cups warm water by hand. Wet hands before making pictures or just playing with the "snowy" mixture.

Encourage children to ask adult family members where they lived when they were children and if they ever played in snow or got "snowed in."

Melting and Freezing

If snow is not available, use small containers of ice shavings for this activity. Model the use of words like *liquid, cold, hot, warm, melt, solid,* and *freeze* as children experiment to find ways to make the snow melt. Might they breathe on the snow, hold the snow in their hands, or put the whole container under a warm coat? If possible, allow children to experience freezing the liquids into solids.

Recognizing Shapes

Place familiar objects, such as a pencil, scissors, or a fork, on an overhead projector. Have children identify each object from its image on the screen.

Innovating on the Poet's Words

Ask what else in the city might turn white when it snows or which of the poem's words would change if snow fell in the country. You might use a transparency of the poem to model adding to the poem or crossing out words to substitute others.

Writing a New Poem

Help children use the poem's ideas and their own to dictate a poem about rain or fog in the city or country at night or in the daytime. Who gets wet? What gets hidden? The repeated line might change to "Got all wet" or "Disappeared."

Reading Related Literature

Share *The Snowy Day* by Ezra Jack Keats, John Burningham's *The Snow*, or Charlotte Zolotow's *Something Is Going to Happen.* Children will enjoy listening to Raffi's snow song, "Douglas Mountain." Read "Thaw," "City," "In the City," "Fog," and "Winter Signs" (all in Related Read-Alouds).

It fell in the city

It fell in the city,
It fell through the night,
And the black rooftops
All turned white.

Red fire hydrants
All turned white.
Blue police cars
All turned white.

Green garbage cans
All turned white.
Gray sidewalks
All turned white.

Yellow No Parking signs
All turned white
When it fell in the city
All through the night.

Eve Merriam

"It fell in the city" from BLACKBERRY INK by Eve Merriam.
Copyright © 1985 by Eve Merriam.
Reprinted by permission of Marian Reiner.

Adventure

Unit 6

1. Satellite

2. My True Story

3. Dressing Up

4. Here Comes the Band

5. Sand

6. Deep in the Forest

7. Whose Shoes

8. Dancing

9. Rides

Purple People Eater

by SHEB WOOLEY

Introducing the Poem
Present the poem dramatically as if you're telling a story that happened to you. Look toward the sky, use one finger as a horn and to point to an eye, look fearful as you shake, and use your hand to show flying movements. Encourage children to join in on the repetitive lines.

Innovating on the Poem's Text
You'll want to use this poem throughout the year as you introduce new colors, numbers, or beginning consonant sounds. Children will love naming and describing new monsters, such as the Yellow Yogurt Eater or Pink Pickle Eater, that may have any number of horns and eyes.

Enjoying Two Meanings
Try wearing purple clothing as you reread the poem. Ask children if they think the monster is purple and eats people or is it a monster that eats purple people? Provide purple paints, paper, and markers for children to illustrate the poem both ways.

Plan a purple day when everyone wears purple to be friendly purple monsters or purple people who make friends with a monster.

Singing the Poem
Once children are familiar with the words, add the music to sing the poem, or play the recording. Tell children that Sheb Wooley wrote the poem's words and the music for the song. Suggest that children share the poem and song at home and see if any family members can sing along.

Popping Up Purple
To make Purple People Eaters that eat purple people, paint recycled tissue paper rolls purple. Invite children to draw faces on purple paper rectangular strips cut to fit inside paper rolls.

Attach these "purple people" to popsicle sticks or straws that push up through the bottoms of the paper rolls. Help children enjoy the repetitive sound of *p* as they play with the pop-ups.

Try writing words that begin with the *p* sound on the purple paper. Encourage children to ask family members at home to help write more "pop-up purple" words.

Welcoming the Purple People Eater
Help children paint, stuff, and join paper bags to make a large Purple People Eater. Use a large button for its eye and recycle a paper towel roll for its horn.

Wrap purple construction paper around rolled up newspaper "logs" or paint paper towel rolls to construct a purple house for the Purple People Eater.

Enjoying Related Literature
Play Heather Bishop's recording, "Purple People Eater," and read "Satellite" (Adventure Poster 1) "Mud Monster" (Me: Theme Opener), *Harry (The Monster)* by Ann Cameron, Maurice Sendak's *Where the Wild Things Are,* and *Amy's Monster* by Jenny Wagner. Children will enjoy Dr. Suess' creatures and their names in *If I Ran the Zoo* and *If I Ran the Circus.*

Activity Page 11: Creating a Monster
Reproduce the page for each child to cut out the parts and create a monster. Encourage children to name their monsters and tell why each is friendly or scary.

Activity Page 12: "Friendly Monster Hat"
Reproduce the page for each child. Help children recite or sing the poem to identify the Purple People Eaters and color them purple. Have children color the other monsters and name them accordingly, such as Violet Violin Eater, Yellow Yucca Eater, Red Rattlesnake Eater. Help children cut out and staple the monster strips to form a circular hat. The 1" extender strip may be used to adjust the hat for the proper size.

See Adding Music, page 180.

The Purple People Eater

Well, I saw the thing
a-comin' out of the sky,
It had one long horn and one big eye.
I commenced to shakin' and I said, "Ooh-wee,
It looks like a purple people eater to me."

It was a one-eyed, one-horned,
Flyin' purple people eater,
One-eyed, one-horned,
Flyin' purple people eater,
One-eyed, one-horned,
Flyin' purple people eater,
Sure looked strange to me.

Well, he came down to earth
And he lit in a tree, I said,
"Mister Purple People Eater,
Don't eat me."
I heard him say in a voice so gruff,
"I wouldn't eat you
'cause you're so tough."

Well, bless my soul, Rock 'n Roll,
Flyin' purple people eater,
Pigeontoed, undergrowed,
Flyin' purple people eater,
He wears short shorts,
Friendly little people eater,

What a sight to see!

Sheb Wooley

Design a Monster

Cut out the monster parts and glue them on another sheet of paper to create a monster. Name the monster and tell what it does that makes it friendly or scary.

126

A Friendly Monster Hat

Color each Purple People Eater purple. Color the other monsters different colors and name them. Cut out the strips and staple them together to make a hat. Add another strip of paper to make it fit, if necessary.

127

Satellite

by OLLIE JAMES ROBERTSON

Previewing Vocabulary

Using the words *revolve* and *orbit*, talk about how you pretend to be a *satellite* like the moon as you move around several children who pretend to be the earth. Model sentences such as "I am the moon/a satellite. I revolve around the earth." Then have a child be the moon who revolves around you as you model sentences such as "I am the earth. The moon/A satellite is in orbit around me." Invite partners to tell about their roles as they take turns being the moon or Earth.

Introducing the Poem

Display the poster and invite discussion about the illustration. Children will enjoy being "moons" that revolve around a globe as you read the poem aloud.

Learning about Artificial Satellites

You may want to share some real and plastic objects such as fruit or flowers to help children compare the moon as a natural satellite to *articifical* satellites that are made by humans and put into orbit for particular purposes. Talk about *weather* satellites that help us learn about the weather or *communications* satellites that receive or send beams so that telephone calls and television or radio programs can be sent or received across the earth. You may also want to talk about other helpful satellites, such as *scientific* satellites that study the air around Earth or *navigation* satellites that work like stars to help sailors and pilots know where they are when at sea or in the air.

Being Artificial Satellites

Have several children join hands and form a circle to play the role of Earth. Reread the poem as other children pretend to be weather satellites who move around "Earth" while reporting on the weather with sentences such as "The sun is shining" or "It's foggy outside." A child from "Earth" might roll or throw a ball to a "communications satellite" who then rolls or throws the ball to the far side of "Earth."

Counting toward "Blast Off"

Invite children to count backwards in unison and then "blast off" as satellites. Encourage children to say the poem with you as you read aloud.

Making Satellites and Space Stations

Talk about *space stations* as larger satellites that are like offices in the sky where several people can work and sleep. Encourage children to use blocks to build satellites or decorate cardboard boxes as specific types of artificial satellites.

Comparing Numbers of Moons

Using a model of the solar system or pictures from encyclopedias and books, compare the number of moons that orbit each planet in our solar system. (Mercury 0, Venus 0, Earth 1, Mars 2, Jupiter 16, Saturn 17, Uranus 15, Neptune 8, Pluto 1) Invite children to play the roles of the planets and their moons.

At other times, help children crumple paper into balls to represent each planet's moons or draw around various round objects to depict the planets and add sticky dots as moons.

Making Space Helmets

Cut off the tops and handles of gallon plastic milk jugs. Children might paint the jugs and glue on stars. Or paint or cover round ice cream cartons with foil and make cut-out windows at eye level.

Enjoying Related Literature

Read and sing "The Family of the Sun" to the tune of "The Farmer in the Dell" and share "Space Satellite" (both in Related Read-Alouds). Share *Astronauts* by Carol Greene, *Regards to the Man in the Moon* by Ezra Jack Keats, *Earthlets, As Explained by Professor Xargle* by Jeanne Willis, *The Moon Dragon* by Moira Miller, or *Space Case* by Edward Marshall.

Satellite

I am a little satellite;
I sparkle with a yellow light.
I orbit round the earth, and then
I speed around and back again.
Beep, beep!
Swish, swish, swish!
Beep, beep!
Swish, swish, swish!
Beep, beep!

Ollie James Robertson

"Satellite" by Ollie James Robertson.
Copyright © 1983 by the Instructor Publications.
Reprinted by permission of Scholastic Inc.

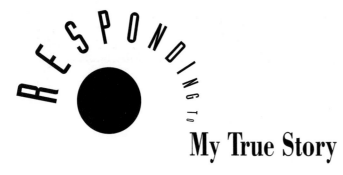

My True Story

by BABS BELL HAJDUSIEWICZ

Setting the Stage

Help children respond chorally to say "that can't be true" or "that can be true" as you present statements, such as "I saw a real dinosaur today," "A boy lost his tooth," or "A mouse pushed me down." Encourage children to initiate more statements.

Introducing the Poem

Before sharing the printless poster, tell children the poem's title and read the poem aloud, helping children join in on the repetitive lines. Then display the poster and invite discussion about the illustration. Help children name the kinds of heads the child dreamed about. You'll want to emphasize that real heads don't come off, but anything can happen in a dream.

For repeated readings, share the recording or present the poem's text on an overhead projector and track the repetitive lines as children join in.

Telling about Dreams

Read *Tar Beach* by Faith Ringold. Invite children to tell about good and bad dreams they've had. Ask what they do when they have bad dreams. Suggest that children ask family members to tell what they do when they have scary dreams.

Share "Covers," "Night Bear," and "I Left My Head" (all in Related Read-Alouds).

Using Logic

Discuss why a person could not buy a head in a store. How about a dinosaur or a smile? Help children draw or cut out pictures to make a chart of things that can and cannot be bought in stores.

Identifying Real and Make-Believe

Stimulate discussion about real and make-believe ideas by reading Selma and Pauline Boyd's *I Met a Polar Bear,* David Wiesner's *Free Fall*, Jan Wahl's *Needle, Noodle and Other Silly Stories*, Hans Christian Anderson's *It's Perfectly True*, and *Why Mosquitoes Buzz in People's Ears: A West African Tale* by Verna Aardema.

Create two-piece puzzles by making horizontal cuts in pictures of animals and objects. Demonstrate joining pieces to make real or silly pictures, such as a lion's head joined to its body or a lion's head joined to the bottom half of a wagon. Encourage children to arrange and rearrange the puzzle pieces on a display with headings such as "This Can Be True" and "This Can't Be True."

Making Faces on Heads

Using peanut butter as "glue," arrange items such as nuts, raisins, vegetables, or marshmallows as features on rice or popcorn cakes. Or use toothpicks to attach paper, felt, or edible features on potatoes.

Creating Self-Portraits

Share Van Gogh's self-portrait and explain that an artist might use a mirror or photograph while creating a self-portrait. Provide a mirror for children to use as they draw their faces. While some children may focus on the primary facial features, others might include details such as eyelashes and freckles. Encourage children to share their self-portraits with family members and then ask family members to pose for portraits.

Comparing Stories

Share James Marshall's *The Three Little Pigs*. Ask children how they think the wolf might tell that story, and then read *The True Story of the Three Little Pigs* by Jon Sciezka. Children might vote on which version they think is true.

Read "The Three Billy-Goats Gruff" or "The Three Bears" from Tomie dePaola's *Favorite Nursery Tales* and then help children tell the goats' story the way the troll might like to tell it or have Goldilocks tell her version of what happened at the Bears' home.

See Meet the Poet, page 189.

My True Story

When I tell my true story to you,
You'll prob'ly say, "That can't be true!"
My head fell off the other day.
    "That can't be true!"
My head fell off and rolled away.
    "That can't be true!"
So I went shopping for a head.
    "That can't be true!"
"We've lots of heads," the store clerk said.
    "That can't be true!"
Then I picked out a head to buy.
    "That can't be true!"
But that head's price was much too high!
    "That can't be true!"
I headed home without a head.
    "That can't be true!"
And there was my head- in my bed!
    "That can't be true!"
My head began to squeal and scream!
    "That can't be true!"
That noise woke me from my bad dream!
    "That CAN be true!"

Babs Bell Hajdusiewicz

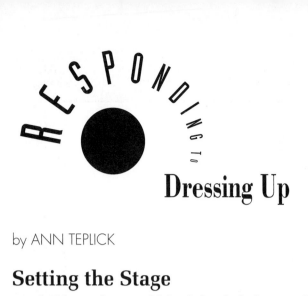

RESPONDING To
Dressing Up

by ANN TEPLICK

Setting the Stage

As children play in old high-heeled shoes, take the opportunity to talk about how each shoe is *long* and *narrow* or *thin* like a *canoe.* Share a picture of a canoe, if need be, and comment on how easy it is to tip a high-heeled shoe over just like it is with a canoe. You might also use a banana to demonstrate the comparison.

Introducing the Poem

Display the poster and read the poem's title. Invite children to stand on their tip toes and wobble, tip, and pretend to trip as you read the poem aloud. Children will enjoy watching themselves in a mirror as they walk on tiptoes.

Making Stilts

Help children use recycled juice cans to make stilts. Punch a hole near the top of each side of the unopened end and thread twine through the holes to make a loop long enough to fit over child's shoulder.

Making Dress-Up Clothes

Groups of three children can take turns being designers, tailors, or models of clothes crafted from fabric scraps, newspapers, or construction paper. Tape a front and back together at child's shoulders and sides. Add sleeves similarly and tie at waist with yarn or ribbon.

To make smocks or fringed vests from paper bags, cut a neck hole in the bottom of a bag and slip over child's head. For a vest, slit the bag down the front, cut arm holes, and cut fringes along the bottom front edges. Children might decorate vests with paint, markers, crayons, or cut-outs.

Sharing Special Dress-Up Times

Read Tomie de Paola's book, *Marianna May and Nursey*, and invite children to tell about times they've gotten all dressed up for special occasions. Ask how it felt to be all "decked out," where they were going, who helped them get dressed, how it felt to have to stay clean, and how it felt to hear compliments from others. Share "I Look Pretty" (Related Read-Alouds).

Making Dress-Up Hats

Share *Old Hat, New Hat* by Stan and Janice Berenstain and then provide materials for children to make all sorts of hats.

To make gathered caps like people wore in Colonial days, punch or cut evenly spaced holes around the edges of fabric circles. Help children weave ribbon or yarn through the holes, pull ends together to gather the circles, and tie the ends in bows.

Add yarn or ribbon ties to recycled materials such as plastic buckets and flowerpots, lampshades, bottoms of gallon plastic jugs, and soccer balls or basketballs cut in half.

Dressing Up for the Day

Plan a special day when children dress up as people they'd like to be. Help children plan and make their clothing for the day. Children will enjoy *Which Witch is Which?* by Pat Hutchins.

At another time, share *Animals Should Definitely Not Wear Clothes* by Judith Barrett and invite children to bring in their favorite stuffed animals to dress up as people.

Dressing Up the Teacher

Invite each child to make one accessory-type item for you to wear. You may want to designate special days when you don children's selections.

Dressing Up a Bulletin Board

Share "Spring" and "In August" (both in Related Read-Alouds). Read Nancy White Carlstrom's *Jesse Bear, What Will You Wear?* or Amy Hest's *Purple Coat.* Then invite children to help divide a bulletin board and label one section for each season in clockwise order. Help children draw or cut out pictures of clothing items they might wear in each season.

Dressing Up

I like wearing
High-heeled shoes!
I stand tall in long canoes.
But when I walk,
I wobble!
I tip!
Oh, gosh! I hope
That I don't trip!

Ann Teplick

"Dressing Up" by Ann Teplick.
Used by permission of the author.

133

Here Comes the Band

by WILLIAM COLE

Building on Prior Knowledge

Read *I Make Music* by Eloise Greenfield. Display pictures of marching bands and individual band instruments, including a tuba, flute, trombone, and trumpet. If possible, invite band members from a local junior or senior high school to show their instruments and demonstrate the sounds.

Introducing the Poem

Display the poster and read the poem's title. Help children identify the instruments in the illustration and then listen for each instrument's name as you read the poem aloud. Reread the poem and pantomime playing each instrument. Invite children to join in to pantomime the actions for repeated readings or as they listen to the recording.

Making Band Instruments

For maracas, fill recycled plastic bottles or film containers with rice, beans, or pennies. Glue two baby food jar lids together with insides facing. Press on the center to make a clacking sound. Coffee cans and oatmeal containers make good drums for wooden-spoon drumsticks. For a tambourine, glue two paper plates together, punch evenly-spaced holes around the edge, and use a large, plastic needle to weave yarn alternately through small bells and holes on plate edges. A tiny rubber band wrapped several times around a bottle cap with serrated edges makes a mini-harp when strummed near the ear. Make percussion sounds with two plain or sandpaper-covered blocks.

Blowing Bottle Music

Help children see how they can produce different sounds by blowing into empty soda bottles and bottles filled with varying amounts of water. Children might arrange the bottles in order by sound.

Marching in the Band

Invite groups to dramatize the poem as band members, baton twirlers, clowns, or the audience who tap their feet and say, "ooh" and "aah." Alternate roles for repeated performances.

At other times, children might recite along with the recording while wearing costumes, carry instruments they've made, or pretend to be the instruments.

Interviewing Family Members

Share Karen Ackerman's *Song and Dance Man* and encourage children to ask family members what, if any, instruments they have played in their lives.

Feeling Different Rhythms

Share books about the effect music can have on feelings. Robert McLoskey's *Lentil* tells the story of a small boy who saves the day with his harmonica when a band can't play in a parade. A band of small children from all over the world has a magical effect in *The Little Band* by James Sage. You may want to have children color or paint as they listen to different types of music.

Invite children to dance or march to the music of recordings such as "Every time I feel the Music," Lisa Atkinson's "The Marching Song," or "Come Follow the Band" by Sharon, Lois, and Bram.

Experimenting with Sound

Fill two film containers each with materials such as sand, rice, beans, cereal, macaroni, and water. Have children shake the containers to match them by sound and then check the contents. Children might also arrange the containers from the loudest to the softest.

Twirling "Ribbons"

Give each child a strip of crepe paper to twirl up, down, left, and right. Children might twirl while marching in single file, two by two, and so on, or twirl according to directions given by a "drum major."

Enjoying Related Literature

Introduce or review "Dancing" (Adventure: Poster 8) or "Ten Tom Toms," "Movement," and "Inside Outside Upside Down" (all in Related Read-Alouds).

See Meet the Poets, page 185

Here Comes the Band

The band comes booming down the street,

The tuba oomphs, the flutes tweet tweet;

The trombones slide, the trumpets blare,

The baton twirls up in the air.

There's "ooh's!" and "ah!" and cheers and

    clapping —

And I can't stop my feet from tapping.

William Cole

"Here Comes the Band" by William Cole.
Used by permission of the author.

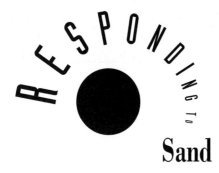
Sand

by JOHN FOSTER

Setting the Stage

Play on the poem's pattern to comment on everyday occurrences. For example, your reaction to a water spill might be, "Water on the tabletop. Water on the floor. Water in the paper cup? Not anymore!" When children are busily tidying (or *should* be), your comment might be any variation of "Blocks in the cupboard. Blocks on the shelves. Blocks in the blocks box. Blocks for busy elves!"

Introducing the Poem

Display the poster and track and read the word *Sand* in the first line. Stimulate interest in the poem's topic and the word's repetition by showing curiosity or amazement in your voice as you track and read the word *Sand* in the second line, and the third, and so on. Then watch children's eagerness to predict the poem's topic *and* read its title! On the first reading, track and chant the words, pausing for children to read the familiar word *Sand* in each line.

Sharing Sandy Experiences

Encourage children to tell about times they've walked or played in sand, where they were, and how it felt to have sand "between your toes" and "everywhere." Ask how sand could get in pajamas or in a bed and how such sandy situations might be prevented. You may want to observe sand grains under a magnifying glass or microscope and share "You can hold" (Related Read-Alouds). Have children experiment with dry and wet paper towels to see when sand clings and when it merely shakes off.

Share Liza Donnelly's *Dinosaur Beach*, Anne Rockwell's and Melanie Greenberg's books, both titled *At the Beach,* or Bruce McMillan's poetic picture book, *One Sun: A Book of Terse Verse.* You may want to introduce or review Shari Lewis' *Baby Lamb Chop Loves the Beach.*

Creating Sand Forms

Have children rub sandstone or other rocks together over black paper. Children might also use sandpaper or sugar cubes.

Provide items such as bottlecaps, blocks with raised letters, cookie cutters, cups, and different kinds of hair combs or combs cut from cardboard. Children will enjoy combining objects to create pictures or molded shapes in wet sand.

Children can blow or fan dry sand on a tray or shallow pan to see how sand dunes or sandstorms occur. To illustrate the formation of a sand bar, have children tilt containers of wet sand or spray water to push sand from one place to another.

Sanding

Provide course, medium, and fine sandpaper squares and unfinished and finished wood blocks in soft and hard woods. Demonstrate use of the materials, and then invite children to experiment to sort woods from soft to hard and sandpapers from course to fine. This is a good time to point out how sandpaper and other objects can change or mar finished surfaces.

Innovating on the Text

Write *SAND* on several sticky tabs and invite children to place the words throughout the room. Help children use each word to begin a sentence such as "*SAND* on the windowpane" or "*SAND* on the coat rack." The resulting list should, of course, end with "*SAND* everywhere!" Repeat the activity to have *Jelly, Snow,* or *Smiles* everywhere! Invite each child to dictate a word you write on sticky tabs to repeat the activity at home.

Painting with Sand

Provide cardboard or heavy paper, glue, and colored sand, if possible. Help children spread glue to form a picture, shape, or their names and then sprinkle sand on the glue.

Children might create a sand painting on the school's sidewalk. Choose a protected area if the weather's effects are of concern, or explain that the Navajo Indians are noted for special sand paintings they create for important ceremonies and destroy afterward.

Sand

Sand in your fingernails
Sand between your toes
Sand in your earholes
Sand up your nose!

Sand in your sandwiches
Sand on your bananas
Sand in your bed at night
Sand in your pajamas!

Sand in your sandals
Sand in your hair
Sand in your trousers
Sand everywhere!

John Foster

"Sand" by John Foster, first published in ANOTHER FIRST
POETRY BOOK (Oxford University Press), included by
permission of the author.

from **Deep in the Forest**

OJIBWAY INDIAN RHYME

Introducing the Poem

Display the poster and read the poem's title. Encourage discussion about the illustration and then ask children to listen to find out what the child sees in the forest in the early morning.

Learning about the Morning Star

Read and sing about the planets in order from the sun in "The Family of the Sun" (Related Read-Alouds). Talk about how Venus and Mercury are closer to the sun than Earth is and how sometimes they reflect sunlight in the eastern sky before sunrise. Explain that long ago, people thought this special morning light was a star so they called it the morning star. You may want to add that when Venus or Mercury reflects light in the western sky after sunset, this light is called the evening star.

Read Alice E. Goudey's *The Day We Saw the Sun Come Up* and *Dawn* by Uri Shulevitz. Encourage children to ask family members to take them out to watch the sun rise or set.

Singing the Poem

Once children have joined you to recite the poem several times, they'll enjoy listening to the familiar words put to music. Invite children to sing along with the first verse on the recording and then listen to more words about the shadows and the morning light. The children might also enjoy singing "Twinkle, Twinkle, Little Star."

Looking into a "Dark Forest"

Help children cover the inside of a cardboard box with black paint. When paint is dry, children can attach glow-in-the-dark stickers or use neon markers to draw stars. Have children use toy objects or draw and cut out animals and trees to create a forest scene inside the box. Hang a dark cloth over the box's opening. Invite children to lift a corner of the cloth and shine a flashlight into the box to peer into the "dark forest."

Enjoying Stars

Share Lenny Hort's *How Many Stars in the Sky?* Read "Satellite," "De Koven," and "from Firefly" (all in Related Read-Alouds).

Share Vincent Van Gogh's painting *Starry Night.* Then provide black paper and invite children to use neon markers and bits of aluminum foil or gold wrapping paper to create their own versions of a starry night.

Make star puzzles for children to assemble. Color and cut out paper stars and cut through the middle of each for five pieces with one point on each.

Making Twinkling Stars

Help children turn an oatmeal box into a "star-making machine." Cover one end of the box with black paper and punch a few holes in the paper. Place a flashlight in the box, point it at the ceiling in a darkened room, and watch the twinkling stars!

Describing Other Places

Help children describe what they might see if they were deep in the jungle, an ocean, a closet or attic, or in outer space.

Camping Out

Share "Sleeping Outdoors" (Related Read-Alouds) and *Sleep Out* by Carol and Donald Carrick. Encourage children who have gone camping to share their experiences. Help children make and hang star mobiles and then use towels or blankets as sleeping bags for a "sleep out" under the stars.

See Adding Music, page 168.

138

from **Deep in the Forest**

Deep in the forest,
dark is the night,
But low in the sky
I see a bright light.

Run, little shadows,
swiftly away!
The bright morning star
is calling the day.

Ojibway Indian

"Deep in the Forest" From AMERICAN PRIMITIVE
MUSIC by Frederick Burton 1909.

Whose Shoes?

by BABS BELL HAJDUSIEWICZ

Introducing the Poem

Display the poster and read the title and poem aloud. Help children use the illustration to answer the poem's questions. Encourage children to tell about times they've played in areas like the one in the picture.

Share related poems such as "Just Watch," "Hoppity," "Heart Beats," "Sliding," or "Merry-Go-Round" (all in Related Read-Alouds).

Dramatizing the Poem

After repeated readings, children will enjoy reciting the poem from memory while acting it out in a gym or outside in a grassy area.

Matching Pairs

Have children remove their shoes, mix them up, and then match the pairs. Provide catalogs and magazines for children to cut out pairs of shoes, separate each pair, and then match them. Glue the pictures on cards to make a Concentration card game.

Making Footprints

Invite children to make footprints in sand or walk with wet feet on a sidewalk. Children will love stepping in paint (and washing up afterwards!) to make footprints on paper. Help children draw around their feet or shoes, cut out the prints, and lay them out to make a path to a special place in the classroom or elsewhere in the building.

Children might ask for help at home to draw around family members' feet or shoes and then arrange footprints in order by size.

Choosing Appropriate Shoes

Read "Shoes" (Related Read-Alouds) and Elizabeth Winthrop's poetic picture book, *Shoes*. Provide clothing and sporting goods catalogs and magazines for children to cut out all sorts of shoes, boots, and slippers. Help children sort the footwear to show which might be worn by men, women, or children, by men *and* women or girls *and* boys, inside or outside, in rain or snow, in warm or cold weather, for various sports, or for jobs such as nursing or firefighting.

Read *The Elves and the Shoemaker* by Paul Galdone and, if possible, visit a shoe repair shop to watch a cobbler at work.

Finding the Shoes That Fit

Provide pairs of shoes and boots in varying sizes, along with shoe and boot boxes in various widths and lengths. Show children how to place a pair of shoes in its box, inside to inside with each toe nested in the other shoe's heel. Children can match pairs of shoes or boots, arrange the footwear by size, find a box to fit each pair, or arrange and stack the boxes by size.

Doing Some Fancy Footwork

Talk about how feet feel when they're in different kinds of shoes or none at all. Have children ask family members about the kinds of shoes their feet like and dislike.

Invite children to wiggle, curl, stretch, and point their toes. Help children find more things that toes and feet can do, such as write or draw pictures or pick up small objects. Share "Feet Only" (Related Read-Alouds) and have children use their feet to pass a soccer ball.

Identifying Animals' Feet

Read *Whose Shoe?* by Margaret Miller and Hana Machotaka's *WHAT NEAT FEET!* Help children count and describe each animal's feet and dramatize how that animal moves. Talk about the shoes a horse wears and, if possible, play a game of horseshoes.

Have partners use pictures of animals and take turns naming the animals from seeing only their feet.

See Meet the Poet, page 189.

Whose Shoes?

Feet in socks go jump!

jump!

jump!

Pairs of shoes piled in a clump.

Jumbled, jumbled, jumbled shoes!

Which shoes are pairs?

Whose shoes are whose?

Babs Bell Hajdusiewicz

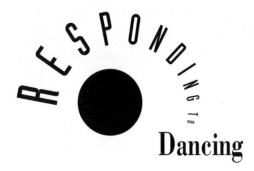

Dancing

by JEANNE B. HARGETT

Introducing the Poem
Display the poster and ask children to listen to the poem to find out what each dinosaur says about dancing. Help children identify the circles and squares in the illustration.

Dancing Around Shapes
Use tape to make a circle and square on the floor. Recite the poem's first stanza as you "dance" around the shapes. Invite children to dance as others join in to recite the stanza or use the tune of "Twinkle, Twinkle, Little Star" to sing new words such as "One side, two sides, three sides, four. Squares have two sides, plus two more" or "Circle, circle, 'round I go. Where I'll stop, I do not know."

Dramatizing the Poem
Make a circular spinner with sections labeled "in a circle," "in a square," "leaping high," "bowing low," "tippy toes," and "tappy heels." Have children take turns spinning to choose how everyone will dance. Children might twirl crepe paper strips as they dance, or sing the poem to the tune of "Twinkle, Twinkle Little Star."

Dancing This Way and That
Dance to circle games such as "The Hokey Pokey" or "Mulberry Bush." For square dancing, have eight children move around a taped square, link elbows, and swing around to "do-si-do." Children might dance with broomsticks or lengths of 40 PVC pipe to Hap Palmer's recording, "Dancing with a Stick."

Making Dancing Puppets
Share poems and pictures in Jane Yolan's *Dinosaur Dances*. Reproduce the dinosaur strip pattern (page 272) for children to color, cut out, and wrap around their fingers. Tape the strips in place so wiggly fingers can make the dinosaurs dance!

For another dancing puppet, fold three identical pictures in half vertically and arrange them so the back sides of the folds meet in the center. Tape together, add legs or arms if desired, and attach string or yarn.

Making Circles and Squares
Provide paper cups and recycled containers for children to trace around. Arrange recycled soda cans to form circles and squares. Cut sponges into shapes, dip in paint, and make shape prints on paper.

Finding Shapes that Roll
Sing "Circles" (Related Read-Alouds) to the tune of "Wheels on the Bus." Then provide square, round, and triangular objects and sing new lines, such as "A triangle block can't roll around..." or "A penny is a circle—it can roll...."

Learning about Special Dances
Share "Cinco de Mayo" and "Movement" (both in Related Read-Alouds) and play a recording of *Swan Lake*. Talk about folk dances, such as clogging, Irish jig, hora, polka, or the flamenco. Encourage children to ask family members to tell about or demonstrate special dances they know.

Making Foods Dance
Place 1 Tbsp baking soda in a clear jar filled with 2 cups water. Add 1 Tbsp raisins and uncooked spaghetti broken into tiny pieces. Add 3 Tbsp vinegar and watch the raisins and spaghetti dance!

Enjoying Related Literature
Share art prints of dancers by Degas. Read "What If..." (Related Read-Alouds), *Dinosaur Dress Up* by Allen L. Sirois, *Dinosaur Bob and His Adventures with the Family Lizardo* by William Joyce, Petra Mathers' *Sophie und Lou,* James Marshall's *The Cut-ups Carry On,* W. Hubbard's *2 is for Dancing,* and Bill Martin Jr.'s *Barn Dance!*

142

Dancing

In a circle
In a square
I like dancing
Anywhere.

Leaping high
Bowing low
Round and round
The room I go.

Tippy toes
Tappy heels
Happy is how
Dancing feels!

Jeanne B. Hargett

"Dancing"(original title "Round and Round") by Jeanne
B. Hargett. Reprinted by permission of the author.

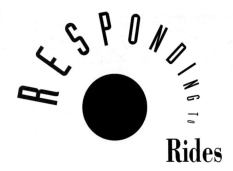

Rides

by ILO ORLEANS

Building on Prior Knowledge

Model using the words *ride, travel, transportation,* and *vehicle* as you talk about which means of transportation you and the children use to get to school each day. Help children make tallies on a chart or attach pictures of feet, cars, buses, and so on to record how each child comes to school. Share *Two Wheels for Grover* by Dan Elliott, and *Fun on Wheels* by Joanna Cole.

Introducing the Poem

Display the poster and ask how the girl in the illustration is traveling. Help children identify each of the vehicles pictured. You may want to talk about ferry boats that carry people and vehicles back and forth across bodies of water. Have children listen to the poem to find out which way the girl likes to travel best.

Dramatizing the Poem

Help groups plan ways to act out riding on each vehicle. At other times, you might use sticky tabs to substitute *We* for *I* on the poster or have children act out the poem while listening to the recording.

Identifying More Ways to Ride

Stimulate thought about more things people ride, such as scooters, skateboards, wagons, roller blades, subways, elevators, various animals, or amusement park rides. Encourage children to tell which rides they have ridden, which they'd like to ride again, and which ones required them to use safety equipment. Then add to or innovate on the poem's text to include children's experiences.

Share "The Trail Ride," a recording by Tom Chapin about the joys of riding a horse, any of Anne Rockwell's books about vehicles, "El Train," "Subway," "Self-Service Elevator," "Alas!" (all in Related Read-Alouds), and sing "Wheels on the Bus."

Riding and Driving

Provide large boxes or riding toys for children's play. Encourage riders and drivers to describe their vehicles and tell where they're going, what safety equipment they're using, how long their trips might take, how many passengers each vehicle holds, and the kind of energy each uses. Introduce or review "Streets," "Signs" (Community: Posters 3 and 8), "Glug! Gurgle! Glug!" (Comunity: Theme Opener), "City Streets," "Circles," "One for Me," and read and sing "Where's My Seat Belt?" (all in Related Read-Alouds).

Exploring What Wheels Do

Help children try to move a box of books or toys and then try moving it on a cart, roller skates, or a skateboard. Talk about why there are wheels under a sofa or refrigerator or on items such as a pizza cutter, tape dispenser, or lawn and garden tools.

Encourage children to ask family members to help identify ways that wheels help them at home.

Experimenting with Motion

Help children use blocks and a board to build an inclined plane and predict which of a group of objects, such as a crayon, block, pencil, jar lid, rolling pin, chalk, marble, or toy car, will roll down the incline and which might just scoot or flop off. Might some objects roll if placed just so? Help children check their predictions. Then raise or lower the inclined plane to see what changes occur.

Counting Wheels on Vehicles

Help children use auto magazines and toy catalogs to cut out pictures of vehicles and group them according to the number of wheels on each.

Making a Steering Wheel

Use a brad fastener to attach a large cardboard circle to the bottom of an oatmeal container. Insert a pencil or small dowel rod through the side of the box for a gear shift.

Preparing Tasty Wheels

Help children cut foods such as bananas, boiled eggs, a cheese or jelly roll, oranges, carrots, and hot dogs into wheel shapes.

Rides

I ride on a bus.
I ride on a train.
I ride on a trolley.
I ride on a plane.
I ride on a ferry.
I ride in a car.
I ride on my skates—
But not very far.
But, best of all,
The ride I like
Is 'round the block
On my new bike.

Ilo Orleans

"Rides" by Ilo Orleans,
reprinted by permission of Karen S. Solomon.

Nursery Rhymes

Unit 7

1. Baa, Baa, Black Sheep

2. Hot Cross Buns

3. Humpty Dumpty

4. Jack and Jill

5. Little Miss Muffet

6. The North Wind Doth Blow

7. Old King Cole

8. Wee Willie Winkie

Baa, Baa, Black Sheep

MOTHER GOOSE RHYME

Introducing the Poem

Display the poster and model showing each number word's value on your fingers as you read the poem aloud. Invite children to join in for repeated readings or to sing the poem's words.

Identifying Animal Sounds

Children will enjoy saying the sheep's sound as you track the words on the poster. Write *sheep* and *baa* in two columns on chart paper under headings of "Animals" and "Sounds." Invite children to say more animals' names and sounds to write. Some children might share words used in other languages. Invite children to draw or cut out animal pictures to add to their list.

You might evaluate children's ability to match animals to their sounds by having one child say an animal's sound and another child ask, "Who said that?" The first child then says, "I am a/an (animal), and I said that!"

Dramatizing the Poem

Provide three small paper bags and stuffing such as black cloth, newspapers, or fiberfill for each group of four children. Talk about the color of a black or white sheep's wool and model the use of the words *full, empty, half-full,* and forms of *heavy* and *light* as children work together to stuff the bags. Help each group decide who will say or sing each character's words to dramatize the poem for others. Exchanging roles to repeat the plays helps children learn all the words for acting out the poem with family members at home.

Try using six bags to build awareness of counting and grouping by twos or threes.

Talking to Communicate

Discuss how each animal has its own unique sound which may be heard when the animal is lonely or content or even hurt, while humans use thousands of different words to say how we think and feel. Have children pretend to be animals who use their sounds to try to express something and then be children who say it in words. Help children discuss how it felt to try to make others understand or to be the listener.

Extend the activity by drawing a pig pen or another animal's house beside a house where people might live. Have children dictate as you write the word for the animal's sound inside the animal's house and words that people say to fill the "people" house.

Sheering "Sheep"

Share Catherine Paladino's *Spring Fleece: A Day of Sheep Shearing.* You might compare the shearing of sheep with people taking their coats off in the springtime or getting haircuts. Talk about how sheep's wool is used to make yarn and fabric for clothing, blankets, and rugs.

Roll whole potatoes in glue and then in cotton and allow to dry. Allow children to use scissors to "shear the sheep."

Enjoying a Related Poem

Display three bags, one containing a sweater, one a rug, and one a blanket. Help children say or sing the poster poem and then repeat the first line. Using the first verse of "Cluck, Cluck, Red Hen" (Related Read-Alouds), pretend to be the sheep and show the contents of each bag. Invite volunteers to take over the sheep's role to repeat the activity. Children will enjoy collecting real or pretend props to act out the other verses of the related poem.

Enjoying More Related Literature

Share "Caballito Blanco," a Spanish song by Sharon, Lois, and Bram that tells about a horse that is asked to carry its rider away to find one sheep for milk, one for wool, and another for butter. Read any of Nancy Shaw's series of books about the adventures of sheep with human characteristics.

See Adding Music, page 166.

Baa, Baa, Black Sheep

Baa, baa, black sheep,
Have you any wool?
Yes sir, yes sir,
Three bags full:

One for my master,
And one for my dame,
And one for the little boy
Who lives in the lane.

Mother Goose Rhyme

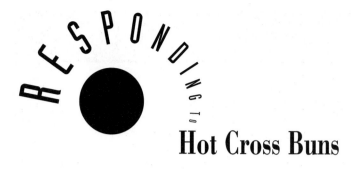

Hot Cross Buns

MOTHER GOOSE RHYME

Building on Prior Knowledge
Talk about buying a sandwich bun at a grocery store, supermarket, bakery, , drug store, convenience store, or from a street vendor. Ask what you might use to make a sandwich if all those stores were out of buns.

Introducing the Poem
Discuss the poster's illustration and read the poem aloud. For repeated readings, track the words on the poster as children recite or sing along with the recording.

Thinking and Reasoning
Use clay to demonstrate that one large bun can be equivalent to two or more smaller buns. Share Laura Joffe Numeroff's books, *If You Give a Moose a Muffin* and *If You Give a Mouse a Cookie* or Pat Hutchins' story, *The Doorbell Rang,* about a family that "stretches" cookies when company arrives.

Invite children to dramatize what a shopper might do with extra buns in a package after eating one for lunch. Ideas might be to keep the buns dry and sealed for later, refrigerate or freeze them, share with others, or buy fewer at a time in the future.

Buying and Selling
Tie yarn shoulder straps to the bottoms of cardboard cartons to make vendors' trays. Children can chant the poem as they take turns being vendors or customers who sell or buy real or clay buns in two sizes. Read and sing "Buy My Flowers" (Related Read-Alouds).

Innovating on the Text
Substitute *nickels, dimes,* or *quarters* for *pennies* and three-syllable word combinations, such as *bagel chips, donut holes,* or *breakfast rolls,* for *hot cross buns.*

Baking Buns
Share Johannes Vermeer's ideas about freshly baked bread in his painting, "A Maidservant Pouring Milk." Try the following recipe to have children make and bake yeast buns.

Place 2 packages dry yeast, 2 cups warm water, and 2 tbsp sugar in a bowl. Do not mix!

Wait five minutes. Then add 2 tsp salt, 2 tbsp *plus* 2 tsp vegetable oil, and 3 cups flour.

Add up to 3 more cups flour to make dough smooth and elastic. Form dough into a ball, place in oiled bowl, and cover with plastic wrap for one hour. Knead dough, shape into buns, and place on oiled baking sheets.

Beat 2 eggs and paint bun tops before baking in 350 ° oven 12 to 15 minutes or until brown.

Publishing Best Bakery Buys
Share Ann Morris' *Bread, Bread, Bread* and, if possible, visit a bakery. Have children dictate sentences, such as "If I went to a bakery, I would buy ..." or "The best food at a bakery is...." Children can add illustrations, a cover, and a title page with their bylines. Bind copies for children to share the bakery guide at home.

Interviewing Family Members
Tell children this poem was written long ago when a penny would buy many kinds of things. Have children ask older family members what they could buy for a penny when they were children.

Making Pennies Count
Help children sort pennies from a group of coins. Try identifying pennies by touch alone. For Presidents' Day, copy Lincoln's image by rubbing the side of a pencil on paper laid over a penny.

Publishing I Can Read Books
Have children illustrate or attach photos of themselves above the words, "I can read" on pages 1, 2, and the last page. The text for the other pages can be words, captions, or brand names children recognize in newspapers or magazines. Sing the book's text to the tune of "Hot Cross Buns."

See Adding Music, page 171.

Hot Cross Buns

Hot cross buns!

Hot cross buns!

One a penny, two a penny,

Hot cross buns!

Mother Goose Rhyme

Humpty Dumpty

MOTHER GOOSE RHYME

Introducing the Poem

Stimulate interest in the poem's topic by asking who had a scrambled, fried, poached, or boiled Humpty Dumpty for breakfast. Tell how you put a Humpty Dumpty in pancakes, cookies, a casserole, or other dish you made recently. Then display the poster and read the poem aloud. Encourage discussion about what Humpty Dumpty is and why he broke and couldn't be fixed. Children enjoy pretending to fall off a wall as they recite or sing the poem's words.

Putting It Together Again

Invite children to color egg shapes cut from cardboard and then cut the shapes into puzzles of two or more pieces. Children might dramatize as they recite or sing the poem and change *couldn't* to *could* as they put Humpty together again. Encourage children to share their puzzles as they recite or sing the poem at home.

Protecting Humpty Dumpty

Use words like *fragile* and *delicate* as you discuss how easily an egg can get broken. This is a good time to share some activities in "Six Speckled Hens" (Animals: Poster 5).

Provide a supply of eggs and packing materials such as newspapers, popcorn, towels, tape, and various containers. Invite children to work together to test ways to keep Humpty Dumpty from breaking in a fall. You might put each test egg in a sealed bag or use boiled eggs. Prepare snacks with broken eggs, and bury shells outside or in potted plants. Or glue shell pieces on egg-shaped cutouts and paint them.

Identifying More Fragile Things

Help children name other things that break easily, such as a spider web, art creations, some jewelry, knick-knacks, or glassware and china. Help children use words like *fix, repair,* and *mend* to talk about which things, if broken, might be put together again by sewing, gluing, nailing, or taping.

Looking for Humpty Dumptys

Recite or sing "Index" (Related Read-Alouds) as you help children find "Humpty Dumpty" in anthologies such as Arnold Lobel's *The Random House Book of Mother Goose*, Volume I of *Childcraft,* or Zena Sutherland's *The Orchard Book of Nursery Rhymes.* Children will enjoy looking for and identifying the words *Humpty Dumpty* and then comparing the illustrations.

Share "Humpty Dumpty," a song by Joe Scruggs, Rodney Peppe's illustrated *Humpty Dumpty,* or introduce children to *Humpty Dumpty's Magazine.*

Changing an Egg's Appearance

Place an egg in a clear jar filled with white vinegar and watch as bubbles cover the shell. Observe for a day to see how the egg floats and sinks as the shell loses its calcium and changes from hard to soft and bouncy.

Constructing a Wall

Provide blocks, dominoes, and other materials such as sugar cubes or recycled cans. Invite groups to build walls and then dramatize the poem using plastic eggs.

Enjoying a Parody or Two

Ask children to listen to another poem about Humpty Dumpty as you recite the poem's first four lines and substitute "Had scrambled eggs for breakfast" for the last line. Ask how this different poem might be illustrated. Using a sentence strip on the poster, show how the new words look and then use sticky tabs to substitute *poached* or *boiled* for *scrambled.* Encourage children to dictate more ideas for parodies of this poem or other nursery rhymes in the collection.

Share "Alas!" (Related Read-Alouds) and then invite discussion about how Jack and Jill would have traveled if *helmet* or *life jacket* were substituted for *seat belt.*

See Adding Music, page 172.

Humpty Dumpty

Humpty Dumpty sat on a wall.

Humpty Dumpty had a great fall.

All the king's horses

And all the king's men

Couldn't put Humpty together again.

Mother Goose Rhyme

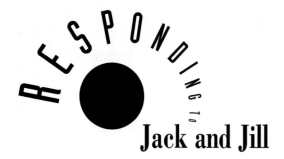

Jack and Jill

MOTHER GOOSE RHYME

Introducing the Poem

Some children will recognize the poem from the poster's illustration and join in as you track the words and read aloud. For repeated readings, you might use hand motions to tell the story or have children sing along with the recorded song.

Using Words with Two Meanings

Explain that the top of a head is called the *crown* just as king's hat is. Help children use each meaning of the word in a sentence. Repeat for other words with two meanings, such as *saw*, *fly*, or *can*.

Dramatizing the Poem

Provide recycled margarine or ice cream tubs or have children bring them from home. Have partners work together to attach yarn handles with tape.

Invite partners to use pails and take turns playing the roles of Jack and Jill. Ask what Jack and Jill might say and do after they fall down, and have children act out a continuation of the story. Play Hap Palmer's recording, "Up and Down a Mountain."

Caring for an Injury

Encourage children to share words such as *owie*, *bump,* or *boo-boo* that they use in their families to describe an injury. Talk about how ice reduces swelling and a bandage keeps an injury clean.

Children might apply a bandage or make an ice pack for a stuffed animal's "injury." Read "Skerbonker Doodles!" (Related Read-Alouds), *Rachel Fister's Blister* by Amy MacDonald, *Maybe a Band-aid Will Help* by Anna Grossnickle Hines, and Bill Martin Jr.'s *Chicka Chicka Boom Boom.*

Innovating on the Text

Help children recognize the rhyming sounds in *hill* and *Jill*, and then think of other names such as *Bill, Will, Gill,* or *Lil* that rhyme. Try substituting each name for *Jill*.

Substitute words like *ran, skipped,* or *crawled* for *went*, and invite children to dramatize each version.

Ask what else Jack and Jill might have gone up the hill to do and substitute phrases such as *pick a bunch of flowers* or *see a pretty sunset*.

Making Comparisons

Provide a meat baster, eye dropper, cup, and spoon for children to explore ways to transfer water from one container to another. Which is quickest? Which is least messy?

Help children experiment outside to find out how much water they can carry in a bucket without spilling it when they walk. How about when they run, crawl, or skip?

Exploring Safety

Read "Alas!" (Related Read-Alouds) and ask children how Jack and Jill went up the hill in this parody. Encourage children to share the poem and talk about the use of seat belts with family members at home.

Compare illustrations that accompany "Jack and Jill" in anthologies such as Volume I of *Childcraft*, Blanche Fisher Wright's *The Real Mother Goose* (originally published in 1916), or *The Random House Book of Mother Goose* by Arnold Lobel. Challenge children to dramatize and then illustrate "Alas!" to show Jill using a seat belt in a car or on an amusement park ride. Then write the poem on chart paper and substitute *helmet* or *life jacket* for *seat belt*. Invite children to illustrate these versions. Share "One for Me" and "Where's My Seat Belt?" (both in Related Read-Alouds) and *Lucky Chuck* by Beverly Cleary.

See Adding Music, page 174.

Jack and Jill

Jack and Jill went up the hill,

To fetch a pail of water;

Jack fell down and broke his crown,

And Jill came tumbling after.

Mother Goose Rhyme

Little Miss Muffet

MOTHER GOOSE RHYME

Introducing the Poem

Display the poster and ask children to predict the poem's topic and title. Children who are familiar with the rhyme will enjoy joining in on the first reading.

Explain that *curds and whey* is similar to cottage cheese and that a *tuffet* is a small clump of grass.

Dramatizing the Poem

Partners can take turns playing the roles of the girl and spider as they recite or sing the poem with you.

You may want to use the poem to evaluate children's understanding of position words. Provide three small toys or blocks to stand for the girl, tuffet, and spider. Invite the child to recite or sing the poem with you while placing the girl *on* the tuffet and the spider *beside* the girl. Then innovate on the text to have the girl sit *near* the tuffet, the spider sit *behind* the girl, and so on.

Learning about Spiders

Introduce or review "If the Spider Could Talk" (Related Read-Alouds) and help children recall what spiders eat, what they make, how many legs they have, and when and why a spider might bite a person.

Take children on a spider hunt in the building and outside. Encourage children to move about carefully to avoid disturbing spiders at work. Afterward, you might help children draw some conclusions about the kinds of places spiders choose to spin webs.

Talking about Fears

Encourage children to talk about why Miss Muffet ran away and what they would do if a spider sat down beside them. Read Ellen Conford's *Eugene*

the Brave to help children recognize that everyone has fears. Suggest that children ask family members about fears they had when they were young children. Share Raffi's song "Spider on the Floor," Barbara M. Joosse's *Spiders in the Fruit Cellar*, and Robert Kraus' *Spider's First Day at School*.

Preparing Spidery Treats

Invite children to make spidery treats using soft oblong rolls for bodies, miniature marshmallows anchored with pretzel pieces for 2, 4, 6, or 8 eyes (most spiders have 8), and pretzel sticks for 8 legs.

Weaving Webs

Tape, scissors, and a ball of string can help turn the opening of a large wastebasket into a web that resembles those made by orb weavers such as the Orange Garden Spider or Marbled Spider. Attach string pieces to resemble wheel spokes and use string, twist ties, or pipe cleaners to make the coiled pattern between the spokes.

On a smaller scale, glue pieces of string on heavy paper to make individual webs or help children use rulers to draw the spokes and use recycled tin cans in graduated sizes as guides for drawing circles to create the coiled look.

Children will enjoy drawing or crafting insects such as grasshoppers, flies, and beetles to place in their webs.

Playing Spidery Ball

Share "Spider, Spider" (Related Read-Alouds) and then invite children to chant the poem as one child pretends to be a spider web that snares one insect for every bouncing ball that's caught.

See Adding Music, page 174.

Little Miss Muffet

Little Miss Muffet
  Sat on a tuffet,
Eating her curds and whey.
  Along came a spider,
And sat down beside her,
  And frightened Miss Muffet away.

Mother Goose Rhyme

The North Wind Doth Blow

MOTHER GOOSE RHYME

Setting the Stage

Invite children to help make and display a large sun and signs that read *North, South, East, West,* and *N, S, E, W.* Build awareness of direction words by leaving the signs on display all year and by including the words in everyday interactions, such as "We'll put this tub of blocks here on the *west* side of the room." Encourage children to ask family members to help make directional signs for a room at home.

Children might make and hold paper suns or pretend to be the sun as they rise from sitting positions on the *east* side of the room and move to sit on the *west* side. You may want to use a compass to check directions.

Building on Prior Knowledge

Read Lois Ehlert's *Feathers for Lunch* and help children identify the robin and other birds in the story. Refer to direction signs as you talk about how birds *migrate* or fly south for warmth in the wintertime.

Share *Animals Don't Wear Pajamas* by Eve B. Feldman and compare the habits and habitats of migrating birds to those of puffins or penguins who love the cold.

Dramatizing the Poem

Introduce the poem by having children gather at the north side of the room to dramatize as you read aloud. Invite three groups to play the roles of the wind, the robin, and a barn. The "wind" might join hands and blow fiercely or fan the "robins" with cardboard or paper. The "barn" can be children who stand in a circle and extend their arms to form an arch-like shelter. "Robins" can "fly" into the barn and tuck heads into their clothing or under their arms.

Display the poster and invite discussion about the illustration. Encourage children to recite and sing along with the recordings.

"Flying South" for Warmth

Invite children to be robins, blue jays, and other migrating birds who shiver and begin flying from the north side of the room to the south side. Encourage children to pantomime getting warmer as they reach the south side.

Introduce or review "Wild Geese" (Animals: Poster 8), "Feathered Letters," and "Who-o-o-o-o Am I?" (both in Related Read-Alouds), and play Raffi's recording, "Robin in the Rain."

Exploring Cold and Warm

Talk about what people do when they feel cold and want to get warm. Include ideas such as finding shelter, adding warm clothing and blankets, rubbing hands together, curling up, hugging others, or moving closer to a source of heat, such as a sunny spot, a heater, or a fireplace. Help volunteers pantomime trying to get warm as others guess what they're doing.

Invite children to hold ice cubes in their hands until they don't enjoy holding them anymore, wave their hands in the air to dry, and then rub their hands together briskly to feel warm again.

Playing "Who's in the Barn?"

Help children list the names of some animals that live in a barn or seek shelter there. Provide a large cardboard box and invite a child to go inside the "barn." Have the child imitate an animal's sound when classmates ask, "Who's in the barn?"

Making Snowy Paperweights

Place tiny pieces of foil in a baby food jar and add liquid detergent until jar is three-quarters full. Add a few drops of glycerine (available at drug and grocery stores) and fill jar to top with water. Tape or glue the lid on and shake to see the "snow" fall.

Using a Word Two Ways

Help children decide whether the word *poor* means the robin is unlucky or has little money. Focus on other homographs or words that look alike but have different meanings, such as *rich* (wealthy/sweet or spicy), *bill* (money owed/bird's beak/hat's brim), or *bat* (flying animal/sporting equipment).

See Adding Music, page 178.

158

The North Wind Doth Blow

The north wind doth blow,
And we shall have snow,
And what will poor Robin do then?
Poor thing.
He'll sit in a barn,
And keep himself warm,
And hide his head under his wing,
Poor thing.

Mother Goose Rhyme

RESPONDING To

Old King Cole

MOTHER GOOSE RHYME

Introducing the Poem

Display the poster and ask children to listen for three kinds of things the king asks for as you read aloud. Children will enjoy playing the roles of the king, the three fiddlers, and those who bring the king's bowl and pipe.

At other times, invite children to recite or sing along with the recording as they dramatize. Children might also act out the poem using their own words, such as "Bring me my bowl" or "We are your fiddlers, your majesty."

Blowing Bubbles

Prepare a bubble solution of one quart warm water, two-thirds of a cup of liquid soap, and one-third of a cup of glycerine (available from grocery and drug stores). Help children cut and flare one end of straws to make bubble pipes.

Making King Cole's Bowl

Show children how to press down in the middle of a ball of clay to mold a bowl. Children might also press or roll out small clay balls, stack the circles, and then press down in the middle to form a bowl.

Filling King Cole's Bowl

List children's ideas about what King Cole might eat from his bowl. Encourage children to use facial expressions as they play-act using a spoon, fork, or chopsticks to eat from a bowl. Can others guess the type of food? Is it a solid or liquid? Is it hot or cold? What utensil is being used?

Constructing a Palace

Read *King Henry's Palace* by Pat Hutchins and Mitsumasa Anno's *The King's Flower*. Provide cardboard boxes and a large area for children to build a *palace* or *castle* fit for a king or queen.

Stack the boxes with open ends facing out so children can decorate and furnish the rooms. Roll colored paper to form cones for steeples, and add flags or streamers.

Creating a Royal Robe

Children will enjoy transforming an old bathrobe into a royal cloak. Use felt, fake fur, fleece fabric, or rolls of cotton stuffing to add collar and cuffs.

Creating a Throne

Provide materials such as crepe paper, ribbons, fabric scraps, bows, and tape for children to transform a chair into a royal throne. Children might wear the royal robe suggested in the above activity and sit on the throne when they have stories or special items to share with classmates.

Writing "Old Queen Cole"

Help children innovate on the poem's text to write about "Old Queen Cole." Using a sticky tab on the poster, substitute *Queen* for *King* in the title. Ask what a queen might "call for" and encourage children to dictate other word substitutions. Make copies for children to share "Old King Cole" and "Old Queen Cole" with family members at home.

Playing with Rhyme

Help children recognize the three rhyming words, *Cole, soul,* and *bowl,* and then name two more words that rhyme with *merry* (berry, cherry, very, Larry), *king* (wing, sing, ring, bring), and *pipe* (ripe, type, wipe, stripe). Write the words on cards and help children group them to make each "rhyming three." Distribute the word cards and invite children to take turns being Old King Cole as he calls for a "Rhyming Three." Encourage children to invite family members to help think of groups of rhyming words.

Sorting Out Real and Pretend

Share Janet Stevens' retelling of Hans Christian Anderson's *The Emperor's New Clothes*. Help children recognize that Old King Cole and the emperor are make-believe kings, while current newspaper articles and photos often tell about real kings and queens.

See Adding Music, page 179.

Old King Cole

Old King Cole

Was a merry old soul,

And a merry old soul was he;

He called for his pipe,

And he called for his bowl,

And he called for his fiddlers three.

Mother Goose Rhyme

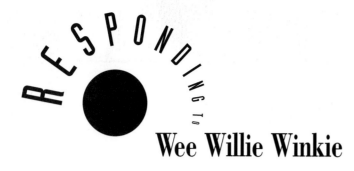

Wee Willie Winkie

MOTHER GOOSE RHYME

Introducing the Poem

Display the poster and read the poem's title. You'll want to dramatize as you read the poem to help children understand the use of the words *rapping* and *crying.*

You may want to tell children that long, long ago, before there were gas or electric lights, it was someone's job to go around and light and then put out the streetlight candles at night. Encourage children to invite family members to go for a walk to see how street lights now go on or off automatically.

Dramatizing the Poem

Invite children to act out the poem with you as you run in place, lift knees high, or bend down as if going up and down stairs, make a knocking motion in the air, and cup your hands to your mouth as if calling out.

Singing the Poem

Have children build stairs with blocks and then move their fingers or toy people up and down the stairs while listening to or singing along with the recorded song.

Telling Time

Make clockfaces using paper plates, cardboard strips for hands, brad fasteners, and numbers cut from newspaper ads. Help children set the hands at eight o'clock before rereading the poem. Then try reciting the poem for other times and reset the hands accordingly. Encourage children to share their clocks and the poem with family members.

Dressing Like Wee Willie

To make a nightcap, roll construction paper into a cone and attach a yarn tassel with a cotton ball on the end. Invite volunteers to wear the cap and an old dress shirt to play the part of Wee Willie as others pretend to sleep.

You may want to explain that long ago before houses had heaters or furnaces, most men, women, and children wore nightshirts and nightcaps to keep warm at night. Children will be interested to know that some people still prefer to wear something warm on their heads when they sleep.

Building Vocabulary

This poem's language and rhythm offer many opportunities for innovating on the text. Model substituting *crawls* for *runs,* and invite children to act out crawling *upstairs and downstairs.* Repeat for other verbs such as *hops, skips,* or *creeps.* Try substituting *small* or *huge* for *wee* and *inside and outside* or *uptown and downtown* for *upstairs and downstairs.*

Using Beginning Consonants

You may want to use this poem as you introduce new consonant sounds. Children whose names begin with a new consonant may substitute their names for *Willie* and add descriptive words that begin with the same sound. Everyone can recite the new words as "Not Noisy Nikki" or "So Super Sammy" plays the part of Wee Willie.

Dramatizing Bedtime

Share *Talk about Bedtime* by Margaret Keen. Talk about how people sleep in order to rest their bodies and have new energy for the next day. Encourage children to talk about and act out bedtime routines such as taking a bath, brushing teeth, gathering up a favorite stuffed animal or blanket, kissing family members goodnight, reading bedtime stories, acting tired when getting into bed, falling asleep.

Enjoying Related Literature

Share "Night Bear" and "Sleeping Outdoors" (both in Related Read-Alouds), *Goodnight Moon* by Margaret Wise Brown, Russell Hoban's *Bedtime for Frances,* and poems from Nancy Larrick's *When the Dark Comes Dancing: A Bedtime Poetry Book.*

See Adding Music, page 181.

Wee Willie Winkie

Wee Willie Winkie
  Runs through the town,
Upstairs and downstairs
  In his nightgown,
Rapping at the window,
  Crying through the lock,
"Are the children in their beds?
  For now it's eight o'clock."

Mother Goose Rhyme

Adding Music

1. Baa, Baa, Black Sheep
2. Beehive
3. Deep in the Forest
4. A Friend
5. Glug! Gurgle! Glug!
6. Hot Cross Buns
7. Humpty Dumpty
8. Jack and Jill
9. Little Miss Muffet
10. Morning Exercises
11. My Bones
12. My Friends
13. The North Wind Doth Blow
14. Old King Cole
15. Purple People Eater
16. Wee Willie Winkie
17. Wild Geese

Baa, Baa, Black Sheep

English Traditional Song

Baa, baa, black sheep, have you an-y wool? Yes, sir, yes, sir, three bags full; One for my mas-ter, and one for my dame, and none for the lit-tle boy who lives in the lane.

Beehive

Words Traditional
Melody by Babs Bell Hajdusiewicz
Accompaniment by Janet Cubic Sima

Deep in the Forest

Ojibway Indian

Quietly

1. Deep in the for - est, dark is the night, But
2. High on the hill and low on the plain The

low in the sky I see a bright light.
warm gold - en sun will soon come a - gain.

Run, lit - tle shad - ows, swift - ly a - way! The
Shad - ows, run quick - ly, run while you may! The

bright morn - ing star is call - ing the day.
bright morn - ing star has called to the day.

A Friend

Words by Betsy Jones Michael
Melody by Babs Bell Hajdusiewicz

It's fun to have a friend!____ Some - one to see and stay with, To walk and talk and play with, To laugh and shout, "Hur - ray!" with. It's fun____ to have____ a friend!_____

Glug! Gurgle! Glug!

Words and melody by Babs Bell Hajdusiewicz
Accompaniment by Janet Cubic Sima

The gas - o - line goes in - to my car. Glug! Gur - gle! Glug!

It makes my car go ve - ry far. Glug! Gur - gle! Glug!

Up - hill, down - hill, up and down. Up - hill, down - hill, up and down.

But sud - den - ly my car won't go. Sput - ter! Sput - ter! Sput!

What is wrong? I do not know! Sput - ter! Sput - ter! Sput!

The oth - er cars a - round me pass. Sput - ter! Sput - ter! Sput! Ah!

I think my car is out of gas! Sput - ter! Sput - ter! Sput!

Hot Cross Buns

Nursery Tune

Hot   cross   buns   Hot   cross   buns

One a pen - ny two a pen - ny hot cross buns.

171

Humpty Dumpty

English Traditional Song

Hump - ty Dump - ty sat on a wall, Hump - ty Dump - ty

had a great fall; All the King's hors - es and all the King's men

Could - n't put Hump - ty to - geth - er a - gain.

Jack and Jill

English Traditional Song

Briskly

Jack and Jill went up the hill, To get a pail of wa - ter;

Jack fell down and broke his crown, And Jill came tum - bling af - ter.

Little Miss Muffet

English Traditional Song

Whimsically

Lit - tle Miss Muf - fet sat on a tuf - fet,

Eat - ting her curds and whey;_____ A - long came a spi - der, and

sat down be - side her, And fright - ened Miss Muf - fet a - way._____

174

Morning Exercises

Words by Babs Bell Hajdusiewicz
Music by Janet Cubic Sima

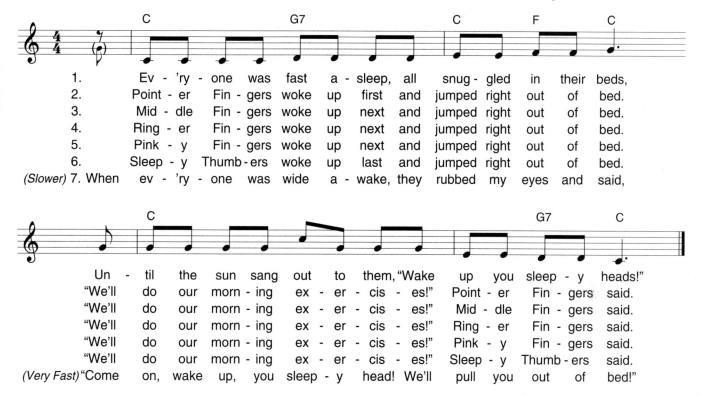

1. Ev - 'ry - one was fast a - sleep, all snug - gled in their beds,
2. Point - er Fin - gers woke up first and jumped right out of bed.
3. Mid - dle Fin - gers woke up next and jumped right out of bed.
4. Ring - er Fin - gers woke up next and jumped right out of bed.
5. Pink - y Fin - gers woke up next and jumped right out of bed.
6. Sleep - y Thumb - ers woke up last and jumped right out of bed.
(Slower) 7. When ev - 'ry - one was wide a - wake, they rubbed my eyes and said,

Un - til the sun sang out to them, "Wake up you sleep - y heads!"
"We'll do our morn - ing ex - er - cis - es!" Point - er Fin - gers said.
"We'll do our morn - ing ex - er - cis - es!" Mid - dle Fin - gers said.
"We'll do our morn - ing ex - er - cis - es!" Ring - er Fin - gers said.
"We'll do our morn - ing ex - er - cis - es!" Pink - y Fin - gers said.
"We'll do our morn - ing ex - er - cis - es!" Sleep - y Thumb - ers said.
(Very Fast) "Come on, wake up, you sleep - y head! We'll pull you out of bed!"

My Bones

Words and melody by Babs Bell Hajdusiewicz
Accompaniment by Janet Cubic Sima

176

My Friends

Words by Sydnie Meltzer Kleinhenz
Music by Mike Kleinhenz

I'm bud - dies with the ba - gel bak - er, Pals with Pearl the piz - za mak - er; Ron - nie brings the mail each day, Bel - sky hauls our trash a - way. Fon - da works at fight - ing fires, Mis - ter Greg re - pairs the wires. Sar - geant So - to says, "Hel - lo." ___ Friends are ev' - ry - where I go. go.

© Modern Curriculum Press. All rights reserved.

The North Wind Doth Blow

Words Anonymous
Melody by Babs Bell Hajdusiewicz
Accompaniment by Janet Cubic Sima

The north wind doth blow, And we shall have snow, And what will poor Rob-in do then? Poor thing. He'll sit in a barn, And keep him-self warm, And hide his head un-der his wing, Poor thing.

Old King Cole

English Traditional Song

Old King Cole was a mer-ry old soul, And a mer-ry old soul was he; He called for his pipe, and he called for his bowl, And he called for his fid - dlers three.

The Purple People Eater

Words and music by Sheb Wooley

1. Well, I saw the thing a-com-in' out of the sky, It had
2. (Well, he) came down to earth and he lit in a tree, I said,

one long horn and one big eye. I com-menced to shak-in' and I
"Mis-ter Pur-ple Peo-ple Eat-er, don't eat me." I heard him say in a

said, "Ooh-wee, it looks like a pur-ple peo-ple eat-er to me."
voice so gruff, "I would-n't eat you 'cause you're so tough."

It was a one-eyed, one-horned, fly-in' pur-ple peo-ple eat-er,
Well, bless my soul, Rock 'n Roll, fly-in' pur-ple peo-ple eat-er,

One-eyed, one-horned, fly-in' pur-ple peo-ple eat-er, One-eyed, one-horned,
Pi-geon toed, un-der growed, fly-in' pur-ple peo-ple eat-er, He wears short shorts,

fly-in' pur-ple peo-ple eat-er, Sure looked strange to me. Well, he
friend-ly lit-tle peo-ple eat-er, What a sight to see.

Wee Willie Winkie

Mother Goose Rhyme
Music by Babs Bell Hajdusiewicz

Wee Wil - lie Win - kie runs through the town,

up - stairs and down - stairs in his night - gown,

rap - ping at the win - dow cry - ing through the lock,

are the child - ren in their beds? For now it's eight o' - clock.

181

Wild Geese

Calmly, but not too slowly

Wild geese, wild geese, fly a - way!
Ka - ri, ka - ri, wa - ta - re!

Big goose a - head as you lead the way;
O - ki - na ka - ri - wa sa - ki - ni;

Small geese be - hind as you
Chi - sa - na ka - ri - wa

fly a - way.
a - to - ni.

Peace - ful - ly, peace - ful - ly fly a - way!
Na - ka - yo - ku wa - ta - ra!

This song may be sung as a two-part round, beginning on indicated numbers 1 and 2.

Meet the Poets

1. Marc Brown

2. William Cole

3. Delia Fira

4. Aileen Fisher

5. Nikki Giovanni

6. Babs Bell Hajdusiewicz

7. Sundaira Morninghouse

8. Carmen Muñoz

9. Anonymous

Marc Brown
(1946-)

Marc Brown always wanted to be an illustrator. When he was a child in Erie, Pennsylvania, his grandmother and uncle gave him lots of paper, pencils, and pens. He loved looking at other artists' work in museums and art books. He liked Marc Chagall's art so much that he changed his name from Mark to Marc.

Marc Brown describes his work as "telling stories in words and pictures." He keeps a drawer full of ideas written on little scraps of paper. He says many of his stories, like *Arthur's Baby,* are about things that have happened to him. He wrote that story when one of his children was born. When he isn't writing or drawing at his home in Massachusetts, Marc Brown likes to read books, fix up old houses, and bake red raspberry pies.

　　　　184

William Cole
(1919-)

William Cole was born in Staten Island, New York. After graduation from high school, he served in the United States Army and then worked as an editor. Besides writing books and poems, William Cole collects and publishes poems written by other poets. As an anthologist, he has published more than forty collections and calls himself a "pack rat" who almost lives in libraries and old book stores when he's searching for poems for a new collection. "Hey! Take a look at *this* one!" he says when he finds a new "gem." When he finishes the anthology, he looks at all those gems and says, "Now they've got a home."

William Cole enjoys playing tennis and ping pong, listening to folk songs, and going to movies in New York, where he lives.

185

Delia Fira
(1946-)

The oldest of thirteen children, Delia Fira grew up on a farm near Corpus Christi, Texas. As a child, she dreamed of being a teacher or singer and of going to see Mount Rushmore. "I saw a picture in a book, and I knew I had to go there to see it for myself." She worked as a mother, a seamstress, and a teacher's assistant before going to college to become a teacher. "Years later, another one of my dreams came true—I went to Mount Rushmore."

Delia Fira enjoys the sounds of words and writes poems in both Spanish and in English. "I like to write about things around me and about things my students wonder about." She lives in Cleveland, Ohio, and enjoys dancing, traveling, lifting weights, and "cooking good food for others to eat."

186

Aileen Fisher
(1906-)

Aileen Fisher lived in the city until she was four years old. Then her family moved to a farm in the country near Iron River on the Upper Peninsula of Michigan. She says she and her brother liked to fish in the river and "skate on it in the winter. We had all kinds of pets—cows, horses, and chickens. And we had a big garden in summer. I loved it. I have always loved the country."

Aileen Fisher likes to write poems about nature because "I enjoy it." She now lives in Boulder, Colorado where she loves being outdoors every day. She says the best part of each day "is a walk with my dog and a friend and her dog on one of the many trails nearby." Aileen Fisher also likes to do woodworking and go hiking and mountain climbing.

187

Nikki Giovanni
(1943-)

Nikki Giovanni was named Yolande Cornelia Giovanni when she was born in Knoxville, Tennessee. When she was a baby, her family moved to Cincinnati, Ohio, where she still lives. Nikki Giovanni writes poems for children and adults and had her first book of poems published when she was twenty-five.

A storyteller, Ms. Giovanni writes both happy poems and sad poems because "I always enjoyed a good story, whether happy or sad." Her poems tell how she feels about things that have happened in her life because, "that's what I know best." Author of *Ego-Tripping and Other Poems for Young People, Vacation Time, and Spin a Soft Black Song,* the poet enjoys music and likes to travel.

Babs Bell Hajdusiewicz
(Hi´-dᴏᴏ-shĕ´-vĭtz) (1944-)

Babs Bell Hajdusiewicz was born in the same house where her parents still live, near Burrows, Indiana. "We didn't have much money when I was a child, so my parents taught us how to make our clothes and toys and almost everything else we wanted or needed." Those early lessons were helpful later when Ms. Hajdusiewicz began teaching and children wanted more of certain kinds of poems or stories—"If I couldn't find what they wanted, I'd write it and ask their opinions. Sometimes they'd say 'Do it again!' and other times they'd tell me how to make the poem or story better."

Besides writing, Babs Bell Hajdusiewicz enjoys reading, traveling, and restoring antiques in Texas where she lives with her husband and two children.

189

Lloyd Wright

Sundaira Morninghouse
(1951-)

Sundaira Morninghouse grew up in Philadelphia, Pennsylvania. She says every holiday was very special for her and her three brothers. "Our aunt, an artist, helped us paint pretty things on all our windows and mirrors." Sundaira Morninghouse still loves to do art projects and especially cottages. She also enjoys dancing, adding to her collection of birds and other winged creatures, studying her family's history, and learning other languages.

When she was in sixth grade, Sundaira Morninghouse wrote her first poem, "but someone else got to read it at graduation because I was chewing bubblegum." A librarian, Ms. Morninghouse lives in Seattle, Washington, with Eartha, her calico cat, who shares her interest in birdwatching.

190

Carmen Muñoz
(1939-)

Carmen Muñoz was born in Roma, Texas, in the Rio Grande Valley. The oldest of seven children, her Saturday chore was to clean the chicken coop on her family's farm. "My favorite thing to do when I finished was to go behind the coop and sit all by myself and watch the hawks fly high in the sky."

Carmen Muñoz planned to be a pharmacist until she discovered how much she enjoyed children while working as a nanny in Chicago. Later, she returned to the Rio Grande Valley to work as a teacher's assistant and then went back to college to be a teacher. Besides writing poems and teaching, Carmen Muñoz enjoys reading, walking, singing Spanish and English songs, and baking upside down cakes at her home in the Valley.

Anonymous

This frame has no picture. That's because we don't know the name of the person who wrote the poem, and we don't know what the person looks like. We say that the poem was written by an anonymous poet.

Related Poems

A Read-Aloud Anthology

RELATED READ-ALOUDS CONTENTS

AFTER A BATH

After my bath
I try, try, try
to wipe myself
till I'm dry, dry, dry.

Hands to wipe
and fingers and toes
and two wet legs
and a shiny nose.

Just think how much
less time I'd take
if I were a dog
and could shake,
   shake, shake.

Aileen Fisher

ALAS!

Jack and Jill
Went up the hill
To fetch a pail of water.
Jack fell down
And broke his crown,
But, alas!
Jill was wearing her seat belt!

Babs Bell Hajdusiewicz

APRIL

Rain is good
for washing leaves
and stones and bricks and even eyes,
and if you hold
your head just so
you can almost see
the tops of skies.

Lucille Clifton

Away floats the butterfly.
To keep it I would never try.

The butterfly's about to 'light;
I would not catch it if I might.

Chinese Rhyme

BABY CHICK

Peck, peck, peck
On the warm brown egg.
Out comes a neck.
Out comes a leg.

How does a chick
Who's not been about,
Discover the trick
Of how to get out?

Aileen Fisher

BED MATE

Whenever lightning strikes at night
   And thunder starts to boom,
My little sister, Ann Marie,
   Comes creeping to my room.

I don't mind moving over
   So there's room for Ann Marie,
I just wish that she would not put
   Her cold feet next to me!

Constance Andrea Keremes

BIRD GARDENS

If birds had gardens,
what would they grow?

Not carrots or beets
or beans in a row,

But weeds, weeds, weeds
to make seeds, seeds, seeds

For birds to eat
in the cold and snow.

Aileen Fisher

BIRTHDAY PIÑATA

WHACK! WHACK! WHACK!
One, two, three.
Fruit, candy, goodies
Falling down on me.

Dancing piñata,
Red and gold;
It's my birthday!
Guess how old.

Celia Sanchez

BIRTHDAY WISH

And after they have sung the song,
       the birthday song,
      the song I know,
The candles sparkle on the cake
And then I get to blow
       and blow—

I stand up
And I take a breath
And blow my way
Around the cake

And all my head is dancing with
The birthday wish I get to make!

Myra Cohn Livingston

BLACKBERRIES

You start out early
Real early in the morning
You cover your arms and legs
From the thorns
The first berries
You drop in your bucket
Go
PLUNK
PLUNK
But you pick some more
Then they make a soft, soft sound
Purple fingers
Purple teeth
One for the bucket
Two for me

Mary Carter Smith

Boa Constricter Boxcars

Oh, I'm being eaten
By a boa constrictor,
A boa constrictor,
A boa constrictor,
I'm being eaten by a boa constrictor,
And I don't like it——one bit.
Well, what do you know?
It's nibblin' my toe.
Oh, gee,
It's up to my knee.
Oh, my,
It's up to my thigh.
Oh, fiddle,
It's up to my middle.
Oh, heck,
It's up to my neck.
Oh, dread,
It's upmmmmmmmmmmmfffffffffff...

Shel Silverstein

Engine, engine on the track
   chugging forward
    chugging back

Boxcar 1 is on the track
   chugging forward
    chugging back

Boxcar 2 is on the track
   chugging forward
    chugging back

Boxcar 3 is on the track
   chugging forward
    chugging back

Boxcar 4 is on the track
   chugging forward
    chugging back

Boxcar 5 is on the track
   All chug forward
    None chug back

Clickety
    Clickety
        Clickety
            Clack!

Gail Blasser Riley

A **B**right red poppy
Can make me feel happy
   And hoppy.
Hop, hip, happy!
Hap, hip, hoppy!
   Poppy!

Mary Q. Steele

BROWNISH-SANDY COTTON CANDY

My hair is cotton—
cotton candy.
Soft, tight curls
but brownish—
sandy.

I fluff it up.
It stays in place.
Soft, fluffed, short hair
hugs my face.

All hugged up
I have to grin.
Hair that hugs me—
outside in.

Lindamichellebaron

BUBBLE TROUBLE?

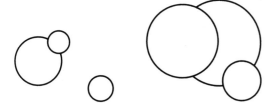

Bubbles, bubbles everywhere
In the tub and in my hair.
Bubbly water, bubbly skin—
What a bubbly world I'm in.

Bubbles, bubbles everywhere
In the water, in the air.
Bubbly walls and bubbly floor,
Bubbly ceiling, bubbly door.

Bubbles, bubbles everywhere
Sure hope Granny doesn't care.
Sure hope Granny likes each bubble.
Sure hope I don't get in trouble!

Babs Bell Hajdusiewicz

BUNNY

Here is a bunny
With ears so funny,
And here is a hole in the ground.

There's a noise Bunny hears!
So he pricks up his ears
And jumps in the hole in the ground!

Anonymous

BUY MY FLOWERS

Oh, won't you buy my sweet
gardenias,
My lovely, fragrant, white gardenias?
Or would you rather buy camelias?
They're rosy red or pink, so fair,
And you can wear them in your hair.
Please buy from me, amigas mias.

María Gonzales

Buy My Flowers

Words and Music by
María Gonzales

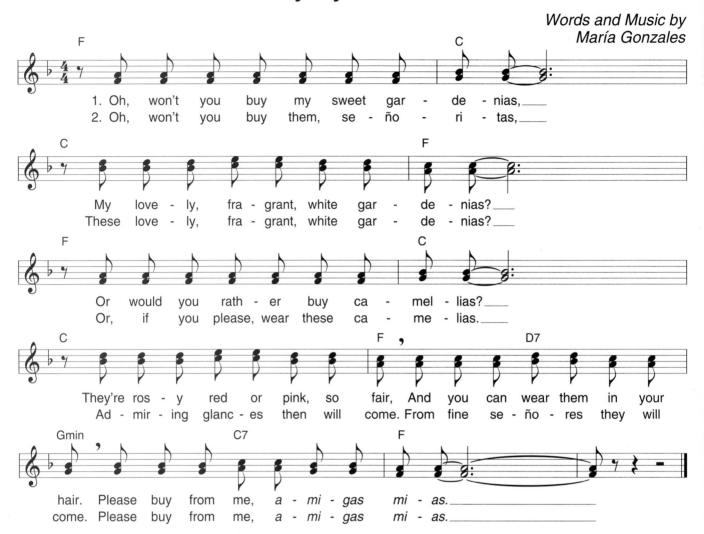

1. Oh, won't you buy my sweet gar - de - nias, ____
2. Oh, won't you buy them, se - ño - ri - tas, ____

My love - ly, fra - grant, white gar - de - nias? ____
These love - ly, fra - grant, white gar - de - nias? ____

Or would you rath - er buy ca - mel - lias? ____
Or, if you please, wear these ca - me - lias. ____

They're ros - y red or pink, so fair, And you can wear them in your
Ad - mir - ing glanc - es then will come. From fine se - ño - res they will

hair. Please buy from me, *a - mi - gas mi - as.* ____
come. Please buy from me, *a - mi - gas mi - as.* ____

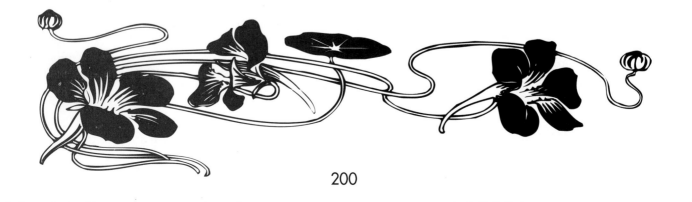

200

BY MYSELF

When I'm by myself
And I close my eyes
I'm a twin
I'm a dimple in a chin
I'm a room full of toys
I'm a squeaky noise
I'm a gospel song
I'm a gong
I'm a leaf turning red
I'm a loaf of brown bread
I'm a whatever I want to be
An anything I care to be
And when I open my eyes
What I care to be
Is me

Eloise Greenfield

CAT

The black cat yawns,
Opens her jaws,
Stretches her legs,
And shows her claws.

Then she gets up
And stands on four
Long stiff legs
And yawns some more.

She shows her sharp teeth,
She stretches her lip,
Her slice of a tongue
Turns up at the tip.

Lifting herself
On her delicate toes,
She arches her back
As high as it goes.

She lets herself down
With particular care,
And pads away
With her tail in the air.

Mary Britton Miller

THE CATERPILLAR

 A caterpillar crawled to the top of a tree.

 "I think I'll take a nap," said he.

 So—under a leaf he began to creep

 To spin a cocoon;

 Then he fell asleep.

 All winter he slept in his cocoon bed,

Till Spring came along one day and said,

 "Wake up, wake up, little sleepyhead.

Wake up, it's time to get out of bed."

So—he opened his eyes that sunshiny day.

Lo! He was a butterfly—and flew away!

Marc Brown

CINCO DE MAYO

Cinco de Mayo, de Mayo, de Mayo!
Cinco de Mayo! Oh my!
Dancing girls whirl and swishy skirts twirl
Caballero clicking heels fly!
Cinco de Mayo, de Mayo, de Mayo!
Cinco de Mayo! Oh my!

Mary Dodson Wade

CIRCLES

(Tune: Wheels on the Bus)
Circles can roll round and round,
Round and round,
Round and round.
Circles can roll round and round
But squares and triangles can't.

Babs Bell Hajdusiewicz

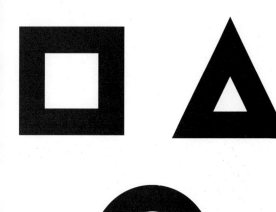

CITY STREET

Honk——honk——honk!
Beep——beep——beep!
Hear the noise
Of city street.

Cars race fast,
Trucks bump past;
Creeping slow
The buses go.

Green turns red,
A sudden stop;
Up the hand
Of traffic cop.

Whistle shrill——
All is still;
Sudden hush——
The people rush.

Red turns green,
Then on again;
Cars race fast,
Trucks bump past.

Lois Lenski

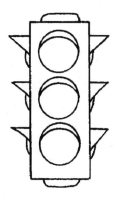

CITY

In the morning the city
Spreads its wings
Making a song
In stone that sings.

In the evening the city
Goes to bed
Hanging lights
About its head.

Langston Hughes

CLICKBEETLE

Click beetle
Clack beetle
Snapjack black beetle
Glint glitter glare beetle
Pin it in your hair beetle
Tack it to your shawl beetle
Wear it at the ball beetle
Shine shimmer spark beetle
Glisten in the dark beetle
Listen to it crack beetle
Click beetle
Clack beetle

Mary Ann Hoberman

Cluck, Cluck, Red Hen

Music Traditional
Adapted lyrics by Jacquelyn Reinach

1. Baa, baa, black sheep, have you an-y wool?

Yes sir, yes sir, three bags full.

One __ for your sweat-er and one for your rug, And one __ for your blan-ket to

keep you warm and snug. Baa, baa, black sheep, have you an-y wool?

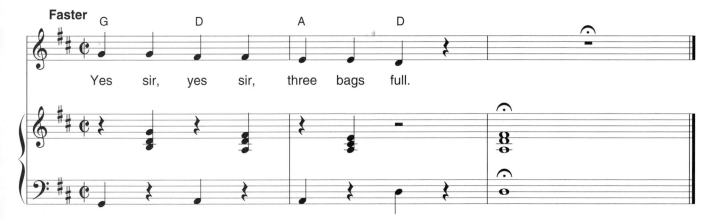

Faster

Yes sir, yes sir, three bags full.

2

Cluck, cluck, red hen, have you any eggs?
Yes sir, yes sir, as many as your legs.
One for your breakfast and one for your lunch,
Come back tomorrow, I'll have another bunch.

3

Moo, moo, brown cow, have you any milk for me?
Yes sir, yes sir, as tasty as can be.
Churn it into butter and make it into cheese,
Freeze it into ice-cream or drink it if you please.

4

Buzz, buzz, busy bee, is your honey sweet?
Yes sir, yes sir, sweet enough to eat.
Honey on your muffin, honey on your cake,
Honey by the spoonful, as much as I can make.

DE KOVEN

You are a dancy little thing,
You are a rascal, star!
You seem to be so near to me,
And yet you are so far.

If I could get you in my hands
You'd never get away.
I'd keep you with me always.
You'd shine both night and day.

Gwendolyn Brooks

COVERS

Glass covers windows
   to keep the cold away
Clouds cover the sky
   to make a rainy day

Nightime covers
   all the things that creep
Blankets cover me

   when I'm asleep

Nikki Giovanni

DIFFERENT
PEOPLE

This person drives a taxi.
This person leads a band.
This person guides the traffic
By holding up a hand.
This person brings the letters.
This person rakes and hoes.
This person is a funny clown
Who dances on tiptoes.

Louise Binder Scott

DRIPPY WEATHER

Geese keep dry
in drippy weather,
oiling feather after feather.

I keep just as dry
. . . and quicker.
I just have to wear my slicker.

Aileen Fisher

EARS HEAR

Flies buzz,
Motors roar.
Kettles hiss,
People snore.
Dogs bark,
Birds cheep.
Autos honk: *Beep! Beep!*

Winds sigh,
Shoes squeak,
Trucks honk,
Floors creak.
Whistles toot,
Bells clang.
Doors slam: *Bang! Bang!*

Kids shout,
Clocks ding.
Babies cry,
Phones ring.
Balls bounce,
Spoons drop.
People scream: *Stop! Stop!*

Lucia and James L. Hymes, Jr.

An earthworm doesn't
make a sound
when he's working
underground.

Lombriz soterrada
trabaja, trabaja
callada, callada.

Ernesto Galarza

EL TRAIN

Riding on the "el" train is lots of fun.
It goes up above the streets
and way down underground.
It sure does make a lot of noise.
It throws electric sparks.
People push and crowd all in;
it says "Screeeeeeeeeeeeeech"
when it stops.

Karama Fufuka

THE ELEPHANT

The elephant goes like this and
    That,
He's terribly big and terribly
    Fat.
He has no fingers, he has no
    Toes,
But goodness gracious, what a
    Nose!

Anonymous

ELETELEPHONY

Once there was an elephant,
Who tried to use the telephant —
No! no! I mean an elephone
Who tried to use the telephone —
(Dear me! I am not certain quite
That even now I've got it right.)

Howe'er it was, he got his trunk
Entangled in the telephunk;
The more he tried to get it free,
The louder buzzed the telephee —
(I fear I'd better drop the song
Of elephop and telephong!)

Laura Richards

EMERGENCY!

If smoke and flames
Are what I see,
I'll stop and think— EMERGENCY!
I'll grab the phone,
Call 911!
I'll ask for help and when I'm done,
I'll run to where
It's safe to stay.
I'll hear that help is on the way————
BE-BOO! BE-BOO! BE-BOO! BE-
BOO! BE-BOO!

Sydnie Meltzer Kleinhenz

Emergency!

Words by Sydnie Meltzer Kleinhenz
Music by Mike Kleinhenz

EVERYBODY SAYS

Everybody says
I look just like my mother.
Everybody says
I'm the image of Aunt Bee.
Everybody says
My nose is like my father's
But *I* want to look like *ME!*

Dorothy Aldis

A FALL OF COLORS

I like sunshine.
I like trees.
I like dancing
In the breeze.

I turn orange.
I turn brown.
I go sailing
To the ground.

I am crispy.
I can crunch.
I get raked up
In a bunch.

I get stuffed
In scarecrow sleeves.
My friends and I
Are AUTUMN LEAVES!

Charles Ghigna

THE FAMILY OF THE SUN
(Tune: The Farmer in the Dell)

The family of the sun, the family of the sun.
Can we name the planets in the family of the
    sun?

Mercury is hot and Mercury is small;
Mercury has no atmosphere. It's just a rocky
    ball.

Venus has thick clouds that hide what is
    below.
The air is foul; the ground is hot; it rotates
    very slow.

We love the earth, our home, its oceans and
    its trees.
We eat its food, we breathe its air, so no
    pollution, please!

Mars is very red. It's also dry and cold.
We'll maybe someday visit Mars. Now
    wouldn't that be bold!

Great Jupiter is big. We've studied it a lot.
We've found that it has fourteen moons
    along with its red spot.

Saturn has great rings— we wondered what
    they were.
But now we know they're icy rocks, though
    once they seemed a blur.

Uranus and Neptune — we don't know
    much about.
In time and with more studying, will we
    know more? No doubt!

Pluto's last in line. It's farthest from the sun.
It's small and cold and icy, too. To land
    there shan't be fun!

The family of the sun, the family of the sun.
Did you count nine planets? Yes, and now
    our journey's done.

Anonymous

208

FEATHERED LETTERS

a **V**
a **Z**
sometimes
a **Y**
That's how
the geese go
flying by.

Sue Thomas

FEET ONLY

A basketball needs both my hands.
A football needs two, too.
But no hands on the soccer ball
'Cause only feet will do.

Babs Bell Hajdusiewicz

FINGER PLAY

One finger
Two fingers
Three fingers
Four
One, two, three, four,
What are fingers for?
Pointing fingers
Crossing fingers
Grabbing fingers, too
Stretching fingers
Hugging fingers
What else can they do?
Bending fingers
Hiding fingers
Need a thumb who's missed,
Thumb lays over
Hiding fingers–
Look!
I've made a fist!

Babs Bell Hajdusiewicz

FROM FIREFLY

I think
if you flew
up to the sky
beside the moon,
you would
twinkle
like a star.

Li Po

FISHY FISHY

(Tune: The Hokey-Pokey)
I put my right fin in
I put my right fin out
I put my right fin in
And I flip myself about
I do the fishy fishy
And I'm swimming all around
That's what it's all about

Babs Bell Hajdusiewicz

FISH WISH

I like this fish, but I wish I could get
A pet that's not wet and cold;
I'd rather have a pet that I
Could kiss and hug and hold.

Yolanda Nave

FIVE LITTLE FISHES

Five little fishes swimming in a pool—
This one said, "The pool is cool."
This one said, "The pool is deep."
This one said, "I'd like to sleep."
This one said, "I'll float and dip."
This one said, "I see a ship."
The fishing boat comes.
The line goes splash.
All the little fishes swim away in a
flash!

Linda Roberts

Fog

Words by Carl Sandburg
Music Anonymous

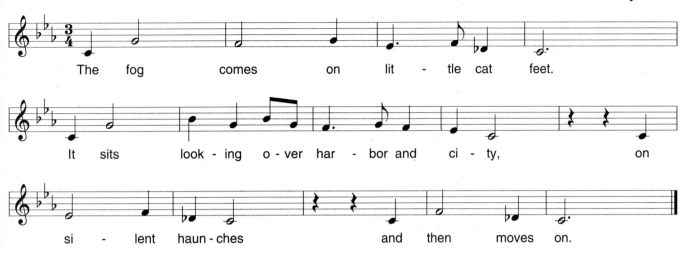

The fog comes on lit - tle cat feet.

It sits look - ing o - ver har - bor and ci - ty, on

si - lent haun - ches and then moves on.

FOG

The fog comes
on little cat feet.

It sits looking
over harbor and city
on silent haunches
and then moves on.

Carl Sandburg

Following me all along the road,
The moon came home
With me tonight.

Kazue Mizumura

FRECKLES

Freckles are speckles,
Quite plain to see
On Ladybug,
Tiger Lily,
Butterfly—
And ME.

Mabel Watts

THE FROG ON THE LOG

There once
Was a green
   Little frog, frog, frog—

Who played
In the wood
   On a log, log, log!

A screech owl
Sitting
   In a tree, tree, tree—

Came after
The frog
   With a scree, scree, scree!

When the frog
Heard the owl—
   In a flash, flash, flash—

He leaped
In the pond
   With a splash, splash, splash!

Ilo Orleans

THE FUNNY HOUSE

We stretched a rope between two trees
And hung a blanket over it.
We pegged the bottom down with stones
And then we crawled inside to sit.

But just as we were playing house,
And starting in to serve some tea,
The funny little house fell down
And covered up my friends and me.

Margaret Hillert

GIANT

I can teach a giant.
I show him what to do
to lift his arms
and kick his feet
and hop as rabbits do.
No matter what I show him
my giant does the same,
because he is my shadow
who even has my name.

Sandra Liatsos

GLUNK, GLUNK, GLUNK

"Ba-rump," went the little green frog.
"Ba-rump," went the little green frog.
"Ba-rump," went the little green frog
        one day,
And his eyes went, "Glunk, glunk,
        glunk!"

Esther L. Nelson

Glunk, Glunk, Glunk

*Words and music by
Esther L. Nelson*

THE GOLDFISH

My funny little goldfish
Hasn't any toes.
He swims around without a sound
And bumps his hungry nose.
He can't get out to play with me
Nor I get in with him.
"Come out and play," I often say,
And he - "Come in and swim."

Anonymous

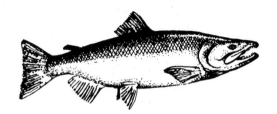

UN ELEFANTE SE BALANCEABA

Un elefante se balanceaba
sobre la tela de una araña,
como veía que resistía
fue a llamar a otro elefante.

Dos elefantes se balanceaban
sobre la tela de una araña,
como veían que resistía
fueron a llamar a otro elefante.

Tres elefantes. . . .
Cuatro elefantes. . . .
Etc. . . .

Mexico

THE GRACEFUL ELEPHANT

One elephant balanced gracefully
Upon a spider's web,
But when the web bounced him all around
He called in another to help hold it down.

Two elephants balanced gracefully
Upon a spider's web,
But when the web bounced them all around
They called in another to help hold it
down.

Three elephants. . . .
Four elephants. . . .
Etc. . . .

Spanish Rhyme

GRAMPS AND I

Gramps and I rocked on the porch one night.
Saw a strange little light in the dark dark night.
We looked to the left
                    And we looked to the right
'Twas nothing but a firefly glowing in the night.

Gramps and I rocked on the porch one night.
Heard a strange little noise in the dark dark night.
We listened to the left
                    And we listened to the right
'Twas nothing but a screen door closing in the night.

Gramps and I rocked on the porch one night.
Smelled a strange little smell in the dark dark night.
We sniffed to the left
                    And we sniffed to the right
'Twas nothing but a tailpipe coughing in the night.

Gramps and I rocked on the porch one night.
And I heard a noise in the dark dark night.
I listened to the left
                    And I listened to the right
'Twas nothing but my grandpa snoring in the night.

Babs Bell Hajdusiewicz

GRIZZLY BEAR

If you ever, ever, ever
        meet a grizzly bear,
You must never, never, never
        ask him where
He is going,
Or what he is doing;
For if you ever, ever dare
To stop a grizzly bear,
You will never
meet another grizzly bear.

Mary Austin

HEART BEATS

My heart beats
    THUMP!
    THUMP!
when I sit.
But when I run,
just listen to it!
    THUMPITY!
    THUMPITY!
    THUMPITY!
    THUMP!

Babs Bell Hajdusiewicz

HINGES

I'm all made of hinges
    and everything bends
From the back of my neck
    way down to the ends.

I'm hinges in front
    and I'm hinges in back.
I'm glad I have hinges
    or else I would CRACK!

Anonymous

215

HOPPITY

Christopher Robin goes
Hoppity, hoppity,

Hoppity, hoppity, hop.
Whenever I tell him
Politely to stop it, he
Says he can't possibly stop.

If he stopped hopping, he couldn't go
    anywhere,
Poor little Christopher
Couldn't go anywhere . . .
That's why he *always* goes
Hoppity, hoppity,
Hoppity,
Hoppity,
Hop.

      A. A. Milne

I AM GROWING!

I am growing
Getting bigger
Getting bigger
Getting bigger
Every day!

      Babs Bell Hajdusiewicz

I DIG, DIG, DIG

I dig, dig, dig,
And I plant some seeds.
I rake, rake, rake,
And I pull some weeds.
I wait and I watch
And soon, you know,
My garden sprouts
And starts to grow.

      Anonymous

I HAD A LITTLE PIG

I had a little pig,
I fed him in a trough,
He got so fat
His tail dropped off.
So I got me a hammer,
And I got me a nail,
And I made my little pig
A brand-new tail.

Anonymous

I LEFT MY HEAD

I left my head
    somewhere
      today.

Put it down for
      just
    a minute.

Under the
    table?
On a chair?

Wish I were
    able
    to say
    where.

Everything I need
    is
    in it!

      Lilian Moore

I Look Pretty

Mama's shiny purple coat
Giant-sized shoulder bag to tote
Tall, tall shoes and pantyhose
Big straw hat with shiny bows
I look pretty
I float
I smile
I pose

Eloise Greenfield

If Only I Could Fly

If only I could fly
If only I were magic
I would soar into the sky.
Oh I would be so happy
I'd never ever cry —
If only only only if
If only I could fly.

Brod Bagert

If the Spider Could Talk

If the spider could talk,
Here are words he might say
To the girl who sat eating
Her curds and her whey:

Hey, Little Miss Muffet!
Come back to your seat!
I'm only out searching
For insects to eat.

Have you seen any grasshoppers?
Beetles or flies?
I'm looking and looking
With all of my eyes.

Come see my eight legs-
Four pairs to your one.
While your legs have bones,
My body has none.

Hey, Little Miss Muffet!
Please don't be afraid.
I'm only a spider.
See the web I have made!

A spider won't bite you
Unless it's afraid
Or injured somehow.
Gosh! I wish you had stayed.

Hey, Little Miss Muffet!
Look! Your curds and whey
Has a fly landing in it-
SLURP! It's my lucky day!

Babs Bell Hajdusiewicz

IN AUGUST

When the sun is strong
   And the day is hot,
We move around
   At a peaceful trot.
We don't wear much
   In the way of clothes
And we squirt ourselves
   With the garden hose.

Marchette Chute

IN THE CITY

The buildings are tall,
The people are small
In the city, in the city.

The noises are loud,
There's always a crowd
In the city, in the city.

The cars move fast,
The trucks jolt past;
Up in the sky the pigeons fly.

East or West,
I like it best
In the city, in the city.

Lois Lenski

IN THE SUMMER WE EAT

In the summer we eat,
in the winter we don't;
In the summer we'll play,
in the winter we won't.
All winter we sleep, each curled in a ball,
As soon as the snowflakes start to fall.
But in spring we each come out of our den,
And start to eat all over again.

Zhenya Gay

INDEX

If I don't know
On which page to look,
I'll use the index
In the back of my book.

Babs Bell Hajdusiewicz

Index

Words by Babs Bell Hajdusiewicz
Music by Susan Burkey

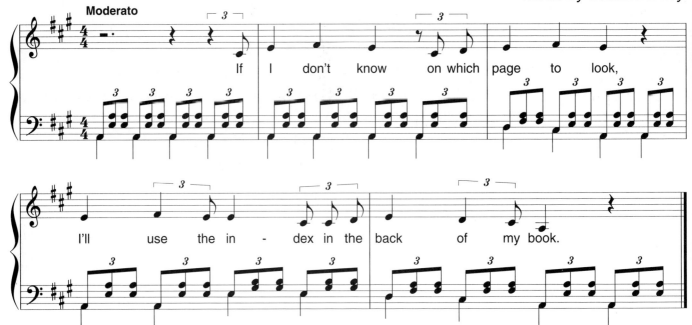

INSIDE OUTSIDE UPSIDE DOWN

Inside Outside Upside Down
Is the funny funny name
Of a funny funny clown
Who walks on his hands
Wherever he goes
And never wears his underwear
Under his clothes.
He wears it on top!
What a funny funny clown
Who's inside, outside, upside-down.

Babs Bell Hajdusiewicz

KEZIAH

I have a secret place to go.
Not anyone may know.

And sometimes when the wind is rough
I cannot get there fast enough.

And sometimes when my mother
Is scolding my big brother,

My secret place, it seems to me,
Is quite the only place to be.

Gwendolyn Brooks

JUST WATCH

Watch
   how high
   I'm jumping,

Watch
   how far
   I hop,

Watch
   how long
   I'm skipping,

   Watch
     how fast
     I stop!

Myra Cohn Livingston

LADY BUG

Lady bug, lady bug,
  Fly away, do!
  Fly to the mountain
  To feed upon dew.

  Feed upon dew
  And when you are through,
Lady bug, lady bug,
Fly home again, do!

Chinese Rhyme

THE LION ROARS WITH A FEARFUL SOUND

The lion roars with a fearful sound,
Roar, roar, roar!

The lion creeps, its prey to catch,
Creep, creep, creep!

The lion pounces with a mighty leap,
Leap, leap, leap!

The lion eats with a crunching sound,
Crunch, crunch, crunch!

The lion sleeps with a gentle snore,
Snore, snore, snore!

Mabel Segun

LITTLE SEEDS WE SOW IN SPRING

Little seeds we sow in spring,
growing while the robins sing,
give up carrots, peas and beans,
tomatoes, pumpkins, squash and
greens.

And we pick them,
one and all,
through the summer,
through the fall.

Winter comes, then spring, and then
little seeds we sow again.

Else Holmelund Minarik

LOOK AT ME!

Two eyes
Two cheeks
One mouth
One nose
See all the ways
I make them pose!

Babs Bell Hajdusiewicz

LOOKING GLASS

It's hard to pass
A looking glass
And not stop
For a minute
To look,
To pause,
And all because
It's *me*
I'm seeing in it.

Leland Jacobs

LUCKY

I'm as lucky as can be
Outside my door there stands a tree

Mary Carter Smith

MAYTIME MAGIC

A little seed
For me to sow . . .

A little earth
To make it grow . . .
A little hole,
A little pat . . .
A little wish,
And that is that.

A little sun,
A little shower . . .
A little while,
And then—a flower!

Mabel Watts

MERRY-GO-ROUND

I climbed up on the merry-go-round,
And it went round and round.
I climbed up on a big brown horse
And it went up and down.
Around and round
And up and down,
Around and round
And up and down,
I sat high up
On a big brown horse
And rode around
On the merry-go-round
    And rode around
On the merry-go-round
I rode around
On the merry-go-round
    Around
        And round
            And
                Round.

Dorothy Baruch

MOOCHIE

Moochie likes to keep on playing
That same old silly game
Peeka Boo!
Peeka Boo!

I get tired of it
But it makes her laugh
And every time she laughs
She gets the hiccups
And every time she gets the hiccups
I laugh

Eloise Greenfield

MOVEMENT

That rock n' roll beat
Makes me move my feet
Hustle
Bump
The Boogaloo
Tomorrow it will be something new
Can't you feel that thump-thump too?

Mary Carter Smith

MR. FROG IS FULL OF HOPS

Mister Frog is full of hops,
'Cause his jumping never stops.
When he leaps he seldom flops.
That's because he's full of hops.

John Schaum

Mr. Frog Is Full of Hops

Words and music by
John Schaum

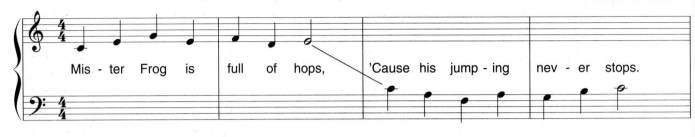

Mis - ter Frog is full of hops, 'Cause his jump - ing nev - er stops.

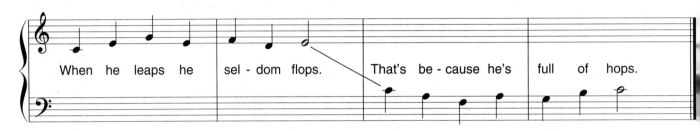

When he leaps he sel - dom flops. That's be - cause he's full of hops.

MY FACES

I can make...
> a funny face
> a sunny face
> a twitchy-nose-like-bunny face
> a pouting face
> a shouting face
> a wondering-and-doubting face
> a sad face
> a mad face
> a feeling-kinda-bad face
> a scary face
> a merry face
> a what-a-sour-berry! face

Whatever face
You see in place
Is my how-I-am-feeling face!

Babs Bell Hajdusiewicz

MY NIPA HUT - BAHAY KUBO

My nipa hut is ever so small,
But the plants in the garden
> are hardy and tall:
See the turnips and peanuts
> and beans in a row
> and spinach and eggplant I grow.

There's radish, squash
> both yellow and white,
And there's mustard and onion
> and lettuce all right,
Ginger, cucumber, cabbage
> and tender green peas,
> Tomatoes and garlic—all these.

Rhyme from Tagalog, Philippines

My Nipa Hut - Bahay Kubo

Tagalog, Philippines

1. Ba - hay ku - bo ka - hi - ma't mun - ti. Ang ho -
1. My ni - pa hut is ev - er so small, But the
2. There's rad - ish, squash both yel - low and white, And there's

la - man do - on ay sa - ri sa - ri.
plants in the gar - den are har - dy and tall:
mus - tard and on - ion and let - tuce all right,

Sing - ko - mos at ta - long, si - gar - ri - llas, ma -
See the tur - nips and pea - nuts and beans in a
Gin - ger, cu - cum - ber, cab - bage and ten - der green

ni, si - too, ba - too, pa - ta - ni.
row and spin - ach and egg - plant I grow.
peas, To - ma - toes and gar - lic— all these.

English by O.S. As sung by Filipino delegation, Athens, Ohio, 1960

MY TEDDY

That teddy bear is mine
I take him everywhere.
But now my friend is loving him
Because I like to share.

Margaret Tapia

Never hug
a Ladybug.
She is agile.
Also fragile.

No abraces
a Mariquita.
La apachurras.
Pobrecita.

Ernesto Galarza

NIGHT BEAR

In the dark of night
when all is still
And I'm half-sleeping in my bed;

It's good to know
my Teddy-bear
is snuggling at my head.

Lee Bennett Hopkins

Noses
are to tell
how roses
smell.

Las rosas tienen
tantos olores
como colores.

Ernesto Galarza

OLD SNAKE HAS GONE TO SLEEP

Sun shining bright on the mountain rock
Old snake has gone to sleep.
Wild flowers blooming round the mountain rock
Old snake has gone to sleep.
Bees buzzing near the mountain rock
Old snake has gone to sleep.
Sun shining warm on the mountain rock
Old snake has gone to sleep.

Margaret Wise Brown

ONE FOR ME

We have five seat belts in our car.
One for Mom
One for Dad
One for Grandma
One for Grandpa
And
One for me.

Babs Bell Hajdusiewicz

THE POET SAYS

A poem is a part of me–
A part of me you do not see.
You see my head
You see my hind
But you can't see what's in my mind.

So I must write that part of me–
The part of me you cannot see.
I take some paper
A pencil or pen
To write what's in my mind and then ...

You have a poem
To read and. . .see!
I've given you
A part of me.

Babs Bell Hajdusiewicz

POP! POPPITY! POP!

POP! POPPITY! POP!
POP! POPPITY! POP!
Pop, poppity, popcorn popped and
    popped!
So I got a bowl and filled it up.
But the POP! POPPITY! POP! POP!
    did not stop.
So I got a tub and filled it up.
But the POP! POPPITY! POP! POP!
    did not stop.
So I got a truck and filled it up.
But the POP! POPPITY! POP! POP!
    did not stop.
So I found the switch and turned it off
And the POP!
           POPPITY!
                POP!
                    POP!
       popped
           and stopped!

Babs Bell Hajdusiewicz

POET UNKNOWN

Some poems are written
By poets who fail
To sign their names
At the end of their tale.

These poets remain
Unknown to us,
So we say their names
Are anonymous.

Babs Bell Hajdusiewicz

THE PRETTY BUTTERFLY

Yesterday I went to the field.
I saw a beautiful butterfly.
But on seeing me so close,
It flew away ever so quickly.

Spanish Rhyme

THE ROOSTER

Cock-a-doodle-doo!
　　The rooster flaps his wings. Cock-a-doodle-doo!
　　He flaps his wings and sings. Cock-a-doodle-doo!
　　The rooster sings, and then Cock-a-doodle!
Cock-a-doodle!
　　　He flaps his wings again.

Anonymous

SATELLITE

Twinkle, twinkle, little star,
Magic eye that sees so far,
Up above the world so high
Taking pictures from the sky!

Doris Parnell Cox

SECRET

Mrs. Kangaroo
Is it true,
Are you hiding
Someone new
In the pocket
Part of you?

There *must* be someone
New and growing,
His little ears
Have started showing.

Beverly McLoughland

SELF-SERVICE ELEVATOR

Buttons,
Buttons,
Buttons,
Lined up in a row—

Push one,
Push one,
Push one,
See where you will go.

Go up,
Go up,
Go up,
Up to the tip-top floor—

Go down,
Go down,
Go down,
Down to the entrance door.

The best thing about a self-service elevator
Is the fun you can have when you're the operator.

Candice Taylor

226

SHADOW ME

I'm your shadow,
Follow me,
Do as I do,
One, two, three.
Clap your hands and lift them high,
Spin them around back to the sky.
Bounce your head from side to side,
Grab your ears and pull them wide.
Stretch your arms and make a yawn,
But close your eyes and I am gone.

Carl Tillmanns

Shadow Me

Chant by Carl Tillmanns

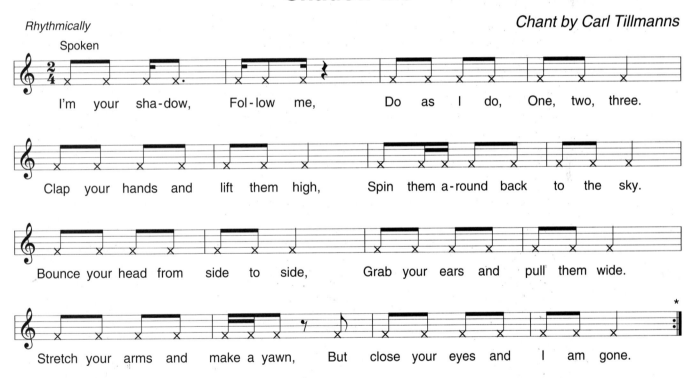

Rhythmically

Spoken

I'm your sha-dow, Fol-low me, Do as I do, One, two, three.

Clap your hands and lift them high, Spin them a-round back to the sky.

Bounce your head from side to side, Grab your ears and pull them wide.

Stretch your arms and make a yawn, But close your eyes and I am gone.

* Repeat two times, each time faster than before.

SHOES

Shoes
Shoes
Shoes
Depend on what you do
Shoes for work
Shoes for play
Shoes for plain old everyday

Rosalyn E. Figge

SKELETON'S CLOTHES

My skeleton likes to stay in.
It's hidden by muscles and skin.
   It wears all its clothes
   From skull down to toes
To keep all its boney bones in.

Babs Bell Hajdusiewicz

SKERBONKER DOODLES!

Skerbonker doodles!
These owies
And oodles
Of boo-boos kept coming my way!
Skerbonker doodles!
My owies
And oodles
Of boo-boos got bandaged today!

Babs Bell Hajdusiewicz

Skerbonker Doodles!

Words and melody by Babs Bell Hajdusiewicz
Accompaniment by Janet Cubic Sima

SLEEPING OUTDOORS

Under the dark is a star,
Under the star is a tree,
Under the tree is a blanket,
And under the blanket is me.

Marchette Chute

SLIDING

Down the slide
We ride, we ride.
Round we run, and then
Up we pop
To reach the top,
Down we come again.

Marchette Chute

SLEEPY FINGERS

My fingers are so sleepy,

It's time they went to bed.

First you, Baby Finger,

Tuck in your little head.

Ring Man, now it's your turn.

Then comes Tall Man great.

Pointer Finger, hurry, because it's getting late!

Let's see if they're all nestled.

No, there's one to come.

Move over, little Pointer,

Make room for Master Thumb!

Marc Brown

SNAIL

Little snail,
Dreaming you go.
Weather and rose
Is all you know.

Weather and rose
Is all you see,
Drinking
The dewdrops
Mystery.

Langston Hughes

SNEEZING

Air comes in tickly
Through my nose,
Then very quickly—
Out it goes:
Ahhh—CHOO!

With every sneeze
I have to do,
I make a breeze—
Ahhh—CHOO!—Ahhh—CHOO!

Marie Louise Allen

SOUNDS

Noise
Hurts my ears
Ambulance screams
Cars honk-honk-honk
Dogs bark
Radios rock
Somewhere
A stereo goes
Beat, Beat, Beat
Up and down the street
I'll get in bed
Pull the cover over my head.

Mary Carter Smith

A SPECIAL DAY

Today the sky
is bluer than ever.
Today the birds
will sing forever.
Today I'll shout
and blow my horn.
Today is the day
that I was born!

Sandra Liatsos

SPECIAL ME

Lots of people have two eyes
Two ears
One mouth
One nose
Two thighs

But no one else has MY two eyes
MY ears
MY mouth
MY nose
MY thighs!

Lots of people have two wrists
Two arms
One neck
One chin
Two fists

But no one else has MY two wrists
MY arms
MY neck
MY chin
MY fists!

I'm special!
ME!
One-of-a-kind!
Another ME you'll never find!

Babs Bell Hajdusiewicz

SPIDER, SPIDER

Spider, spider,
Spin your web,
Catching insects
In your thread.
How many insects can you catch?
One, two, three . . .

Anonymous

SPRING

How pleasing—
not
to be
freezing.

Prince Redcloud

STOP SIGN'S SONG

(Tune: I'm a Little Teapot)

I'm a traffic stop sign
on patrol.
I warn all the people
from my pole.

When I'm at a corner,
I say STOP!
S   T   O   P
STOP!
STOP!
STOP!

Babs Bell Hajdusiewicz

STOP, DROP, AND ROLL

I'd STOP, STOP, STOP.
I'd DROP to the ground.
I'd ROLL, ROLL, ROLL
All around and around.

If my clothes were on fire,
I'd drop to the ground.
I'd STOP, DROP, and ROLL
All around and around.

Mary Dodson Wade

STOP, LOOK, LISTEN

We'll stop
We'll look
We'll listen
Before we cross the street.
We'll use our eyes
We'll use our ears
And then we'll use our feet!

Anonymous

SUBWAY

Down
Down
Down
Down
Under the ground
Rumble
Rumble
Rumble
Rumble
What's that sound?
Whoosh-a
Rumble
Whoosh-a
Rumble
Zoom
Zoom
Zoom
The subway train is zooming
through its underground room

Babs Bell Hajdusiewicz

SUN FUN

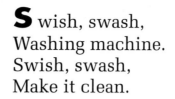

The sun went down
and took away
my shadow friend.
He's gone away.
He won't come back
Until...
Unless...
Tomorrow's full of sunniness!

Babs Bell Hajdusiewicz

S wish, swash,
Washing machine.
Swish, swash,
Make it clean.

Swish, swash,
Bubble and spin.
Swish, swash,
Pack it all in.

Mishmash,
Jeans and sheets,
T-shirts and towels,
And a skirt with pleats.

Mishmash,
Three odd socks,
An old rag doll,
And a terry-cloth fox.

Swish, swash,
Washing machine.
Swish, swash,
Clean all clean.

Eve Merriam

TEN TOM-TOMS

Ten tom-toms,
Timpani, too,
Ten tall tubas
And an old kazoo

Ten trombones–
Give them a hand!
The sitting-standing-marching-running
Big Brass Band

Anonymous

THANKSGIVING

I feel so stuffed inside my skin
And full of little groans,
I know just how the turkey felt
Before it turned to bones.

Margaret Hillert

THIS TOOTH

I jiggled it
    jaggled it
      jerked it.

I pushed
   and pulled
   and poked it.
But —

As soon as I stopped,
and left it alone,
This tooth came out
on its very own!

Lee Bennett Hopkins

THAW

The snow is soft,
   and how it squashes!
"Galumph, galumph!"
   go my galoshes.

Eunice Tietjens

THUMB SAYS

Four fingers bragged that they could do
Most anything they wanted to.
They said mean things and laughed at Thumb
Who stood there
       all alone
          and glum.

But one day Thumb had heard enough,
"You fingers think that you're so tough!
You brag about what you can do.
Well, I'll show YOU a thing or two!
You say I'm short and kinda fat,
But who helps you put on a hat?
And who helps you to grab a ball
Or hug a teddy bear or doll?
And who helps you to make a fist?"
Then
    Thumb and Fingers
         hugged and kissed!

Babs Bell Hajdusiewicz

TO CATCH A FISH

Dana went to catch a fish
He took his fishing pole
And cast his line into the lake
A chocolate cookie was his bait
He sat upon a rock to wait
To catch a great big fish

Suddenly he heard Blub Blub
Two fish stuck out their heads
"Offer us our favorite dishes
Worms or flies or smaller fishes
Maybe then you'll get your wish"
And off they swam, Blub Blub!

Nanette Mellage

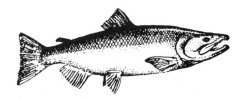

235

TOASTER TIME

Tick tick tick tick tick tick tick
Toast up a sandwich quick quick
quick
Hamwich
Jamwich
Lick lick lick!

Tick tick tick tick tick tick- Stop!
POP!

Eve Merriam

TOMMY

I put a seed into the ground
And said, "I'll watch it grow."
I watered it and cared for it
As well as I could know.

One day I walked in my back yard,
And oh, what did I see!
My seed had popped itself right out,
Without consulting me.

Gwendolyn Brooks

TOWER OF BLOCKS

Building up a tower of blocks.
Down it flops
if someone knocks!

John Schaum

Tower of Blocks

*Words and music by
John Schaum*

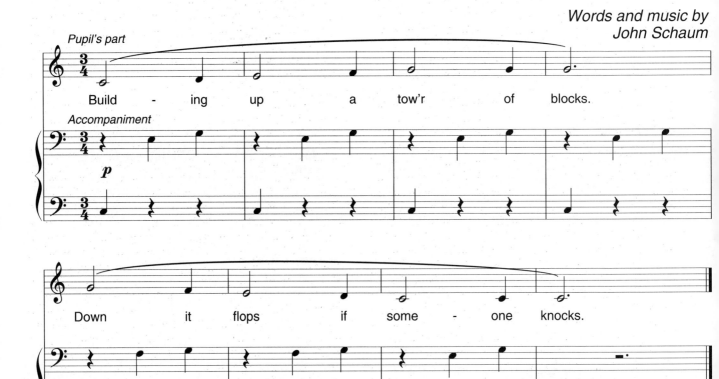

TOY TIK KA

I like fish. Toy tik ka.
I like chicken. Toy tik ga.
I like duck. Toy tik veet.
I like meat. Toy tik teet.
But though I like ka, ga, veet, teet—
Fish and chicken, duck and meat—
Best of all I like to eat.

Charlotte Pomerantz

TRAFFIC LIGHT

Traffic light, traffic light
   Red
   Yellow
   Green
       Top
       Middle
       Bottom
I know what they mean!

Red at the top
Says STOP! STOP! STOP!
Red light, red light,
STOP! STOP! STOP!

Yellow in the middle
Says WAIT! WAIT! WAIT!
Yellow light, yellow light,
WAIT! WAIT! WAIT!

Green at the bottom
Says GO! GO! GO!
Green light, green light,
GO!
       GO!
            GO!

Babs Bell Hajdusiewicz

THE TRAIN

"To Caracas," says the train
   when it's coming from Los Teques."
To Caracas, to Caracas,
   swiftly over hills and ridges,
Sometimes passing through a tunnel,
   sometimes passing over bridges.

When it passes through a tunnel,
   it goes slowly, very slowly;
With great care it passes slowly
   so the folk will not be scary;
Slowly, slowly, very slowly,
   no more hurry, very wary.

When the bridges are behind,
   then it goes a little faster;
Faster, faster, much much faster,
   to Caracas without stopping:
See the houses, see the city,
   now we're braking, now we're
       stopping.

Venezuelan Folktune
translated by Mary S. de Saettone

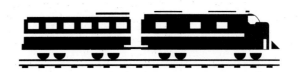

The Train
El Tren

Words Anonymous
English by Mary S. de Saettone
Folktune from Venezuela

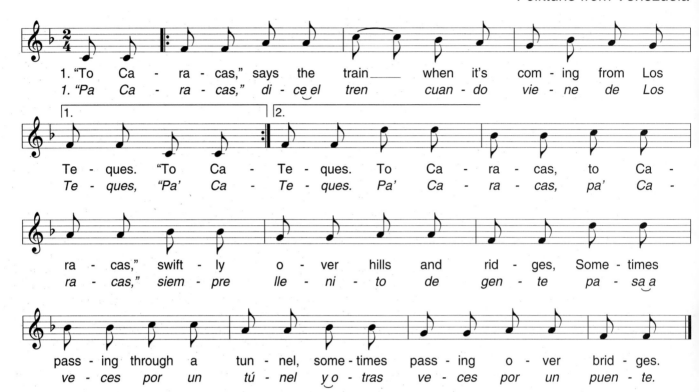

1. "To Ca - ra - cas," says the train____ when it's com - ing from Los
1. "Pa Ca - ra - cas," di - ce el tren cuan - do vie - ne de Los

Te - ques. "To Ca - Te - ques. To Ca - ra - cas, to Ca -
Te - ques, "Pa' Ca - Te - ques. Pa' Ca - ra - cas, pa' Ca -

ra - cas," swift - ly o - ver hills and rid - ges, Some - times
ra - cas," siem - pre lle - ni - to de gen - te pa - sa a

pass - ing through a tun - nel, some - times pass - ing o - ver brid - ges.
ve - ces por un tú - nel y o - tras ve - ces por un puen - te.

2. (Slowly)

When it passes through a tunnel,
it goes slowly, very slowly;
With great care it passes slowly
so the folk will not be scary;
Slowly, slowly, very slowly,
no more hurry, very wary.

3. (Faster, then slower)

When the bridges are behind,
then it goes a little faster;
Faster, faster, much, much faster,
to Caracas without stopping;
See the houses, see the city,
now we're braking, now we're stopping.

TURKEY GOBBLER

The barnyard turkey
is a wise old bird
Who talks
    GOBBLE-GOBBLE
and wishes to be heard!
He spreads
    GOBBLE-GOBBLE
his tail like a fan
And struts
    GOBBLE-GOBBLE
as he shares his plan:
"In November
    GOBBLE-GOBBLE
when you have a feast,
Let me
    GOBBLE-GOBBLE
be your centerpiece beast.
But don't
    GOBBLE-GOBBLE
take my feathers away!
And don't
    GOBBLE-GOBBLE
serve me sliced on a tray!
Instead
    GOBBLE-GOBBLE
let me sit there alive
And be handsome
    GOBBLE-GOBBLE
when your guests arrive!
If you'll
    GOBBLE-GOBBLE
serve your feast MY way,
We'll ALL
    GOBBLE-GOBBLE
have a thanks-giving day!"

Babs Bell Hajdusiewicz

TURTLES

When turtles hide within their shells
There is no way of knowing
Which is front and which is back
And which way which is going.

John Travers Moore

Two little sisters went walking one day,
Partly for exercise, partly for play.
The took with them kites which they
wanted
    to fly,
One a big centipede, one a great butterfly.
Then up in a moment the kites floated
high,
Like dragons that seemed to be touching
    the sky!

Chinese Rhyme

VACUUM

Vroom! Vroom! Vroom!
Vroom! Vroom! Vroom!
Vroom goes the vacuum
All around the room!

Vroom, vroom forward!
Vroom, vroom back!
Vroom, vroom vacuum's
    on a
D I R T   A T T A C K !

Babs Bell Hajdusiewicz

VALENTINE FEELINGS

I feel flippy,
I feel fizzy,
I feel whoopy,
I feel whizzy.

I'm feeling wonderful.
I'm feeling just fine.
Because you just gave me
A valentine.

Lee Bennett Hopkins

WALKING

I stop—
    it stops, too.
It goes when I do.

Over my shoulder I can see
The moon is talking a walk with me.

Lilian Moore

Watching the full moon,
a small hungry boy forgets
    to eat his supper.

Basho

WE'LL EAT TURKEY

(Tune: Where is Thumbkin?)

We'll eat turkey
We'll eat turkey
Oh, so good!
Oh, so good!
For Thanksgiving dinner
For Thanksgiving dinner
Mmm-mmm good!
Mmm-mmm good!

Anonymous

WHAT IF. . .

What if. . .
    You opened a book
    About dinosaurs
And one stumbled out
And another and another
    And more and more pour
Until the whole place
Is bumbling and rumbling
And groaning and moaning
    And snoring and roaring
And dinosauring?

What if. . .
    You tried to push them
    Back inside
But they kept tromping
Off the pages instead?
    Would you close the covers?

Isabel Joshlin Glaser

WHEN I GROW UP

When I grow up
Who will I be
Besides the person
Who is ME?
I might bring mail
I might play drums
I might drive trucks
I might grow plums
I might fight fires
I might trim trees
I might type letters
I might mend knees
When I grow up
Who I will be
Is a worker who works
But I'll still be ME!

Babs Bell Hajdusiewicz

WHERE'S MY SEAT BELT?

(Tune: Where is Thumbkin?)

Where's my seat belt?
Where's my seat belt?
Here it is.
Here it is.
Watch how I can hook it!
Watch how I can hook it!
Now I'm safe!
Now I'm safe!

Babs Bell Hajdusiewicz

WHO HAS SEEN THE WIND?

Who has seen the wind?
Neither I nor you;
But when the leaves hang trembling,
The wind is passing through.
Who has seen the wind?
Neither you nor I;
But when the trees bow down their heads,
The wind is passing by.

Christina Rossetti

Who Has Seen the Wind?

Words by Christina Rossetti
Music by L.E. Wann

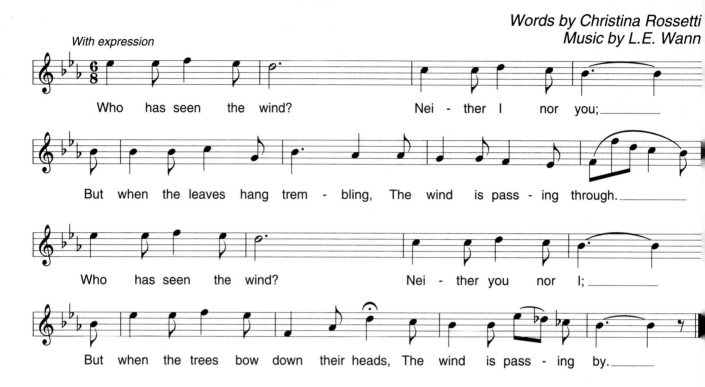

With expression

Who has seen the wind? Nei - ther I nor you;

But when the leaves hang trem - bling, The wind is pass - ing through.

Who has seen the wind? Nei - ther you nor I;

But when the trees bow down their heads, The wind is pass - ing by.

WHO-O-O-O-O AM I?

Who-o-o-o-o am I
    who shakes new blossoms off the trees?
Who-o-o-o-o am I
    who snatches hats off heads with ease?
Who-o-o-o-o am I
    who chases litter down the street?
Who-o-o-o-o am I
    who tries to whip you off your feet?
Who-o-o-o-o am I
    who lifts dry leaves on autumn days?
Who-o-o-o-o am I
    who helps the moon make ocean waves?
Who-o-o-o-o am I
    who shows the bushes how to dance?
Who-o-o-o-o am I
    who dries your dripping shirts and pants?
I am the wind-
That's **who-o-o-o-o-o-o**!

Babs Bell Hajdusiewicz

 # WINTER SIGNS

Winter signs are everywhere,
the winter winds are nipping,
winter snow is in my hair,
my winter nose is dripping.

Jack Prelutsky

THE WORRIED CATERPILLAR

Caterpillar, don't you worry
If your body's fat and furry.
Please remember, by and by -
You'll be a lovely butterfly.

Marilyn Collett

WOULDN'T YOU?

If I
Could go
As high
And low
As the wind
As the wind
As the wind
Can blow—

I'd go!

John Ciardi

YES OR NO

Sometimes I say YES, I'LL GO,
But sometimes I say NO! NO! NO!

YES if my daddy says, "Come inside."
But NO if a stranger says, "Come for a ride."
YES if my friend says, "Let's go play."
But NO if a stranger says, "Don't run away."
YES if my mommy says, "Let's go see."
But NO if a stranger says, "Talk to me."
YES if my auntie says, "Come in and eat."
But NO if a stranger says, "Come have a treat."

Sometimes I say YES, I'LL GO,
But sometimes I say
NO!
    NO!
        NO!

Babs Bell Hajdusiewicz

YESTERDAY'S PAPER

Yesterday's paper makes a hat,
   Or a boat,
   Or a plane,
   Or a playhouse mat.
Yesterday's paper makes things
   Like that—
   And a very fine tent
   For a sleeping cat.

Mabel Watts

YOU

I like shadows
I like sun
I like you
more than anyone.

I like summer
I like the cold
I'll even like you
when you're old.

I like work
I like play
I like you
    every which way.

Charlotte Zolotow

You can hold
in your hand
millions and billions and
trillions of sand.

Grano con grano
en la mano llena
miles y biles y triles
de granos de arena.

Ernesto Galarza

243

Zoo

The zoo has everything—
Animals galore
You could never buy
In any store:

Pandas and zebras,
Goats and apes,
Lions and tigers
And cobras with capes,

Wolves and hyenas,
Elephants, bears,
And proud sea lions
That walk up stairs!

John Travers Moore

YOUR SHADOW SAYS

I am you
but bigger than you
and longer than you
and darker than you

You are me
but smaller than me
and shorter than me
and afraid of me.

J. Patrick Lewis

Indexes

INDEX - AUTHORS

INDEX - AUTHORS

INDEX - AUTHORS

INDEX - FIRST LINES

INDEX - FIRST LINES

INDEX - FIRST LINES

INDEX - TITLES

INDEX - TITLES

INDEX - TITLES

INDEX - CURRICULUM CONNECTIONS

Page numbers indicate where activities related to various curriculum areas are located in the Idea Book.

INDEX - CURRICULUM CONNECTIONS

Page numbers indicate where activities related to various curriculum areas are located in the Idea Book.

INDEX - CURRICULUM CONNECTIONS

Page numbers indicate where activities related to various curriculum areas are located in the Idea Book.

Social Studies

INDEX - CURRICULUM CONNECTIONS

Page numbers indicate where activities related to various curriculum areas are located in the Idea Book.

INDEX - CURRICULUM CONNECTIONS

Page numbers indicate where activities related to various curriculum areas are located in the Idea Book.

INDEX - FAMILY INVOLVEMENT

INDEX - LITERATURE, ART, & MUSIC CONNECTIONS

Isadora, Rachel. *I Touch.* Greenwillow, 1985. 24

Joosse, Barbara M. *Spiders in the Fruit Cellar.* Knopf, 1983. 156

Joslin, Sesyle. *What Do You Say, Dear?/What Do You Do Dear?* Harper, 1958. 34

Joyce, William. *Dinosaur Bob and His Adventures with the Family Lizardo.* Harper, 1988. 142

Keen, Margaret. *Talk about Bedtime.* Ladybird Books from Talkabout Series, 1977. 162

Keller, Holly. *Lizzie's Invitation.* Greenwillow, 1987. 28

Kellogg, Steven. *Can I Keep Him?* Dial, 1971. 84

Kraus, Robert. *Leo the Late Bloomer.* Simon & Schuster, 1987. 94

—. *Spider's First Day at School.* Scholastic, 1987. 156

Lionni, Leo. *It's Mine.* Knopf, 1986. 74

—. *Swimmy.* Random House, 1968. 84

Lobel, Arnold. *Frog and Toad Are Friends.* Harper, 1970. 28

—. *Frog and Toad Pop-Up Book.* Harper, 1986. 88

—. *On Market Street.* Greenwillow, 1981. 70

MacDonald, Amy. *Rachel Fister's Blister.* Houghton Mifflin, 1990. 72

Marshall, James. *George and Martha.* Houghton Mifflin, 1972. 28

—. *The Cut-ups Carry On.* Viking, 1990. 142

Martin, Bill Jr. and John Archambault. *Barn Dance!* Holt, 1986. 142

Mathers, Petra. *Sophie and Lou.* Harper, 1991. 142

McClosky, Robert. *Make Way for Ducklings.* Viking, 1941. 98

McLeod, Emily. *Bear's Bicycle.* Little, Brown, 1975. 104

McMillan, Bruce. *One, Two, One Pair.* Scholastic, 1991. 140

Numeroff, Laura Joffe. *If You Give a Moose a Muffin.* Harper, 1991. 80

—. *If You Give a Mouse a Cookie.* Harper, 1985. 80

Oxenbury, Helen. *Shopping Trip.* Dial, 1982. 70

Parish, Peggy. *Amelia Bedelia.* Harper, 1963. 18

—. *Amelia Bedelia and the Baby.* Greenwillow, 1981. 18

—. *Amelia Bedelia and the Surprise Shower.* Harper, 1966. 18

—. *Amelia Bedelia Helps Out.* Greenwillow, 1979. 18

—. *See and Do Books.* Greenwillow, 1980. 30

Parker, Nancy Winslow and Joan Richards Wright. *Bugs.* Morrow, 1988. 80

Peppe, Rodney, illust. *Humpty Dumpty.* Viking Kestrel, 1976. 152

Piper, Watty. *The Little Eengine That Could.* Platt & Munk, 1930. 62

Pluckrose, Henry. *Tasting.* Franklin Watts, 1986. 24

Riddell, Chris. *The Trouble with Elephants.* J.B. Lippincott, 1988. 86

Rockwell, Anne and Harlow. *Happy Birthday to Me.* Macmillan, 1981. 22

Rogers, Fred. *Making Friends.* Putnam, 1987. 68

Rohmer, Harriet. *Uncle Nacho's Hat/El Sombrero del tio Nacho.* Children's Book Press, 1989. 22

Scarry, Richard. *Cars and Trucks and Things That Go.* Western, 1974. 48

Sharmat, Marjorie. *I'm Not Oscar's Friend Any More.* Dutton, 1975. 28

Sharmat, Mitchell. *Gregory, the Terrible Eater.* Four Winds Press, 1980. 34

Shaw, Nancy. *Sheep in a Jeep.* Houghton Mifflin, 1986. 148

—. *Sheep in a Shop.* Houghton Mifflin, 1991. 148

—. *Sheep on a Ship.* Houghton Mifflin, 1989. 148

Showers, Paul. *Listening Walk.* HarperCollins, 1991. 24

Shulevitz, Uri. *Dawn.* Farrar, 1974. 138

Sirois, Allen L. *Dinosaur Dress Up.* Tambourine, 1992. 142

Tudor, Tasha. *First Delights: A Book About the Five Senses.* Putnam, 1988. 24

Watanabe, Schiego. *I Can Build a House.* Philomel, 1985. 30

—. *How Do I Put It On?* Putnam, 1990. 68

—. *I Can Ride It.* Philomel, 1988. 30

—. *I Can Take a Walk.* Philomel, 1985 30

Wiesner, David. *Tuesday.* Clarion, 1991. 98

Winthrop, Elizabeth. *Shoes.* Harper, 1988. 140

Wiseman, Bernard. *Morris and Borris.* Putnam, 1988. 18

—. *Morris and Borris at the Circus.* Harper, 1988. 18

—. *Morris Goes to School.* Harper, 1983. 18

—. *Morris Has a Cold.* Scholastic, 1990. 18

—. *Morris the Moose.* Harper, 1989. 18

Ziefert, Harriet. *Max and Diana and the Shopping Trip.* Harper, 1987. 70

INDEX - Literature, Art, & Music Connections

Magazine

Humpty Dumpty's Magazine. Benjamin Franklin Literary and Medical Society, Inc., Box 567, 100 Waterway Blvd., Indianapolis IN 46206.   152

Recordings

Annie. Columbia, CIK-3800, JST 3800, 1977.   26

Chapin, Tom. "Good Garbage." *Mother Earth.* A & M Records, 75021, 04132, 1990.   64

Chapin, Tom. "Happy Birthday." *Moonbeat.* Sundance Music, Inc., CS0403, 1989.   22

Disney Records. "Under the Sea." *The Little Mermaid.* Buena Vista Records. DIS 606 184.   84

Makin' Music. "Over in the Meadow." *Playsongs and Games.* Musical Munchkins, 1989.   90

Palmer, Hap. "Dancing with a Stick." *Sally the Swinging Snake.* Activity Records, 1987.   142

Raffi and Ken Wheatley. "Five Little Frogs." *Singable Songs for the Very Young.* Troubadour Records, SL 0202-A, 1977.   88

Raffi. *More Singable Songs.* Troubador Records, SL 0202-A, 1979.

—. "Robin in the Rain." *Singable Songs.* Troubador Records, SL0202-A, 1977.   158

—. "Sharing Song." *Singable Songs.* Troubador Records, SI0202-A, 1977.   74

—. "Spider on the Floor." *Singable Songs.* Troubador Records, SL 0202-A1977, 1977.   156

Rosenshontz. Rosen, Gary and Bill Shontz."Garbage." *Share It.* RS 82-02, 1982.   64

Scruggs, Joe. "Humpty Dumpty." *Bahama Pajamas.* Educational Graphics Press, Inc., SPR 250,1990.   152

Sharon, Lois, and Bram. "Chicken Medley." *Sharon Lois and Bram Sing A to Z.* Elephant Records, 1990.   92

—. "Five Little Fishes." *Sharon, Lois, and Bram Sing A to Z.* Elephant Records, 1990.   84

Tchaikovsky. *Swan Lake, Op. 20, Leonard Bernstein Conductor.* CBS Records, MT 30056.   142

Works of Art

Conner, Patrick. *People at Work.* Looking at Art Series. Atheneum, 1982.

Degas prints. Newlands, Anne. *Meet Edgar Degas.* Lippincott, 1989.   142

The Thinker. Hale, William H. *The World of Rodin.* Time Inc., 1969.   30

Van Gogh's self portrait. Measham, Terry. *Van Gogh and His World.* Great Masters Series. Silver Burdett, 1980.   138

Van Gogh, Vincent. *Starry Night* Peter, Adeline and Ernest Raboff. *Art for Children Series: Vincent Van Gogh.* Doubleday.   138

ACKNOWLEDGMENTS

Every reasonable effort has been made to locate the ownership of copyrighted materials and to make due acknowledgment. Any errors or omissions will gladly be rectified in future editions.• "A bright red poppy" from ANNA'S SUMMER SONGS by Mary Q. Steele. Text copyright © 1988 by Mary Q. Steele. By permission of Greenwillow Books, a division of William Morrow & Company, Inc. • "A Fall of Colors" by Charles Ghigna Originally published in TURTLE MAGAZINE, copyright © 1991 by Children's Better Health Institute, Benjamin Franklin Literary and Medical Society, Inc., Indianapolis, IN. Used by permission of the author. • "A Friend" by Betsy Jones Michael. Reprinted by permission of the author. • "A House Is a House For Me" by Mary Ann Hoberman. Copyright © 1978 by Mary Ann Hoberman. Used by permission of Viking Penguin, a division of Penguin Books USA Inc. • "A Special Day" by Sandra Liatsos. Copyright © 1991 by Sandra Liatsos. Reprinted by permission of the author's agent, Marian Reiner. • "After a Bath" by Aileen Fisher from UP THE WINDY HILL © 1953. Copyright renewed. Reprinted with permission of the author. • "Alas" © 1987 by Babs Bell Hajdusiewicz. Reprinted by permission of the author. • "All About Me" by Donna Lugg Pape. Reprinted by permission of the author. • "April" from EVERETT ANDERSON'S YEAR by Lucille Clifton. Copyright © 1974 Lucille Clifton. Reprinted by permission of Henry Holt & Company, Inc. • "Away floats the butterfly" from CHINESE MOTHER GOOSE RHYMES selected & edited by Robert Wyndham, copyright © 1968 by Robert Wyndham. Reprinted by permission of Philomel Books. • "Baby Chick" by Aileen Fisher from RUNNY DAYS, SUNNY DAYS © 1953, copyright renewed 1986. Reprinted by permission of the author. • "Bed Mate" by Constance Andrea Keremes. Reprinted by permission of the author. • "Beehive" Melody by Babs Bell Hajdusiewicz. Accompaniment by Janet Cubic Sima. •"Bird Gardens" by Aileen Fisher. Reprinted by permission of the author, Aileen Fisher. • "Birthday Wish" from BIRTHDAY POEMS by Myra Cohn Livingston (Holiday House) Copyright © 1989 by Myra Cohn Livingston. Reprinted by permission of Marian Reiner for the author. • "Blackberries," "Lucky" and "Movement" from TOWN CHILD by Mary Carter Smith. Copyright © 1966, 1971, 1976 by Mary Carter Smith. Reprinted by permission of the author. • "Boa Constrictor" from WHERE THE SIDEWALK ENDS by Shel Silverstein. © 1974 by Evil Eye Music, Inc. Selection reprinted by permission of HarperCollins Publishers. "Boxcars" © 1991 by Gail Blasser Riley. Reprinted by permission of the author. • "Brownish-Sandy Cotton Candy" © 1989 Lindamichellebaron. Reprinted by permission of Linda Baron Dudley. • "Bubble Trouble?" © 1988 by Babs Bell Hajdusiewicz. Reprinted by permission of the author. • "Buy My Flowers" by María Gonzales from Singing Together of OUR SINGING WORLD, © Copyright, 1959, 1957, 1951, by Ginn and Company. Used by permission of Silver Burdett Ginn Inc. • "By Myself" from HONEY, I LOVE by Eloise Greenfield. Text copyright © 1978 by Eloise Greenfield. Selection reprinted by permission of HarperCollins Publishers. • "Cat" by Mary Britton Miller. Copyright, estate of Mary Britton Miller. Reprinted by permission of James N. Miller. • "Chucka-chucka Choo-choo" by Sundaira Morninghouse. Reprinted by permission of Carletta Wilson. • "Cinco de Mayo" by Mary Dodson Wade. Used by permission of the author. • "Circles" © 1989 and "Copycat" © 1992 by Babs Bell Hajdusiewicz. Reprinted by permission of the author. • "City" by Langston Hughes. Reprinted by permission of Harold Ober Associates Incorporated. Copyright © 1958 by Langston Hughes. Copyright renewed 1986 by George Houston Bass. • "City Street" by Lois Lenski © 1954 from WE LIVE IN THE CITY. Used by permission of The Lois Lenski Covey Foundation, Inc. • "Clickbeetle" by Mary Ann Hoberman. Reprinted by permission of Gina Maccoby Literary Agency. Copyright © 1976 by Mary Ann Hoberman. • "Cluck, Cluck, Red Hen" Adapted lyrics by Jacquelyn Reinach. Copyright

© 1970 by Childways Music (ASCAP) . Used by permission. • Text of "Covers" from VACATION TIME: Poems for Children by Nikki Giovanni. Text Copyright © 1980 by Nikki Giovanni. By permission of William Morrow & Company, Inc. • "Dancing"(original title "Round and Round") by Jeanne B. Hargett. Reprinted by permission of the author. • "De Koven" from BRONZEVILLE BOYS AND GIRLS by Gwendolyn Brooks Copyright © 1956 by Gwendolyn Brooks Blakely. Selection reprinted by permission of HarperCollins Publishers. • "Deep in the Forest" From AMERICAN PRIMITIVE MUSIC by Frederick Burton 1909. • Excerpts from "Different People" from RHYMES FOR LEARNING TIMES by Louis Binder Scott © 1983 T.S. Denison and Company Inc. Minneapolis, MN Reprinted by permission of publisher.• "Dinner Time" by Leslie D. Perkins. Used by permission of the author. • "Dressing Up" by Ann Teplick. Used by permission of the author. • "Drippy Weather" by Aileen Fisher. Reprinted by permission of the author, Aileen Fisher. • "Ears Hear" by Lucia & James Hymes, Jr., Oodles of Noodles, © 1964 by Addison-Wesley Publishing Company, Inc. Reprinted with permission of the publisher. • "El Train" from MY DADDY IS A COOL DUDE AND OTHER POEMS by Karama Fufuka. Copyright © 1975 by Karama Fufuka. Used by permission of Dial Books for Young Readers, a division of Penguin Books USA Inc. • "Elephant" diagrams by Marc Brown from PLAY RHYMES by Marc Brown. Copyright © 1987 by Marc Brown. Used by permission of Dutton Children's Books, a division of Penguin Books USA Inc. •"Eletelphoney" from TIRRA LIRRA: RHYMES OLD AND NEW by Laura Richards. Copyright © 1930, 1960 by Laura Richards. Copyright © renewed 1960 by Hamilton Richards. By permission of Little, Brown and Company. • "Emergency" Lyrics by Sydnie Meltzer Kleinhenz. Music by Mike Kleinhenz. Used by permission. • "Everybody Says" by Dorothy Aldis reprinted by permission of G.P. Putnam's Sons from HERE, THERE & EVERYWHERE by Dorothy Aldis, copyright 1927, 1928, copyright renewed © 1955, 1956 by Dorothy Aldis. • "Feathered Letters" by Sue Thomas. Used by permission of the author, who controls all rights. • "Feet Only" © 1991 and "Finger Play" © 1991 by Babs Bell Hajdusiewicz. Used by permission of the author. • "Fighting Makes No Sense" © 1991 by Babs Bell Hajdusiewicz. Reprinted by permission of the author. • " The Firefly" by Li T'ai Po (second stanza) Reprinted from A GARDEN OF PEONIES, translated by Henry H. Hart with the permission of the publishers, Stanford University Press. Copyright © 1938 by the Board of Trustees of the Leland Standford Junior University. Copyright renewed 1966 by Henry S. Hart. • "Fish Wish" from GOOSEBUMPS AND BUTTERFLIES by Yolanda Nave. Copyright © 1990 by Yolanda Nave. Reprinted with permission of the publisher Orchard Books, New York. • "Fishy Fish" © 1989 by Babs Bell Hajdusiewicz. Reprinted by permission of the author. • "Five Little Fishes" by Lynda Roberts from MITT MAGIC: FINGERPLAYS FOR FINGER PUPPETS ©1985 by Lynda Roberts. Reprinted by permission of Gryphon House Inc. • "Fog" from CHICAGO POEMS by Carl Sandburg, copyright 1916 by Holt, Rinehart and Winston, Inc. and renewed 1944 by Carl Sandburg, reprinted by permission of Harcourt Brace Jovanovich, Inc. • "Following Me All Along the Road" from FLOWER MOON SNOW: A BOOK OF HAIKU by Kazue Mizumura. Copyright © 1977 by Kazue Mizumura. Selection reprinted by permission of HarperCollins Publishers. • "Freckles" by Mabel Watts. Reprinted by permission of Patricia Linda Babcock for the author. • "Froggie, Froggie" from CHINESE MOTHER GOOSE RHYMES selected & edited by Robert Wyndham, copyright © 1968 by Robert Wyndham. Reprinted by permission of Philomel Books. • "Giant" by Sandra Liatsos. Copyright © 1992 by Sandra Liatsos. Used by permission of the author's agent, Marian Reiner. • "Glug, Gurgle, Glug" © 1986 and "Gobble! Gobble! Munch!" © 1991 by Babs Bell Hajdusiewicz. Reprinted by permission of the author. • "Glunk, Glunk, Glunk" reprinted by

Acknowledgments

permission of Sterling Publishing Co., Inc., 387 Park Ave. S., NY, NY 10016 from THE FUNNY SONGBOOK by Esther L. Nelson, © 1984 by Esther L. Nelson. • "Goldie" by Margaret Tapia. Used by permission of the author. • "Goops" by Gelett Burgess. • "Gramps and I" © 1991 by Babs Bell Hajdusiewicz. Reprinted by permission of the author. • "Grandpa" by Jean Parker Katz. Used by permission of the author. • "Grizzly Bear" from THE CHILDREN SING IN THE FAR WEST by Mary Austin. Copyright 1928 by Mary Austin. Copyright © renewed 1956 by Kenneth M. Chapman and Mary C. Wheelwright. Reprinted by permission of Houghton Mifflin Company. All rights reserved. • "Happy Birthday to Me!" by Carmen Muñoz. Used by permission of the author. •"Heart Beats" © 1991 by Babs Bell Hajdusiewicz. Reprinted by permission of the author. • "Here Comes the Band" by William Cole. Used by permission of the author. • "Hey Bug!" from I FEEL THE SAME WAY by Lilian Moore. Copyright © 1967 by Lilian Moore. Reprinted by permission of Marian Reiner for the author. • "Hiding" by Dorothy Aldis reprinted by permission of G.P. Putnam's Sons from EVERYTHING AND ANYTHING by Dorothy Aldis, copyright 1925, 1926, 1927, copyright renewed 1953, 1954, 1955 by Dorothy Aldis. • "Hoppity", from WHEN WE WERE VERY YOUNG by A.A. Milne. Copyright 1924 by E.P. Dutton, renewed 1952 by A.A. Milne. Used by permission of Dutton Children's Books, a division of Penguin Books USA Inc. • " I Am Growing" © 1989 and "I Can" © 1990 by Babs Bell Hajdusiewicz. Reprinted by permission of the author. • "I Left My Head" from SEE MY LOVELY POISON IVY by Lilian Moore. Copyright © 1975 by Lilian Moore. Reprinted by permission of Marian Reiner for the author. • "I Like You" reprinted with permission of Charles Scribner's Sons, an imprint of Macmillan Publishing Company, from I LIKE YOU AND OTHER POEMS OF VALENTINE'S DAY. Selected and illustrated by Yaroslava. Copyright © 1976 by Yaroslava Surmach Mills. • "I Look Pretty" and "I love" from HONEY, I LOVE by Eloise Greenfield. Text copyright © 1978 by Eloise Greenfield. Selection reprinted by permission of HarperCollins Publishers. • "If Only I Could Fly" by Brod Bagert. Used by permission of Boyds Mills Press, Honesdale, PA Copyright © 1992. • "If the Spider Could Talk" © 1989 by Babs Bell Hajdusiewicz. Reprinted by permission of the author. • "I'm Sharing" and "In the Tub" by Lada Josefa Kratky. Used by permission of the author. • "In August" from Around and About by Marchette Chute, copyright 1957 by E.P.Dutton. Copyright renewed 1984 by Marchette Chute. Reprinted by permission of Elizabeth Roach. • "In the City" by Lois Lenski © 1954 from WE LIVE IN THE CITY. Used by permission of The Lois Lenski Covey Foundation, Inc. • "In the Summer We Eat", from BITS AND PIECES by Zhenya Gay. Copyright © 1958 by Zhenya Gay, renewed © 1986 by Erika L. Hinchley. Used by permission of Viking Penguin, a division of Penguin Books USA Inc. • "Index" © 1989 and "Inside Outside Upside Down" © 1991 by Babs Bell Hajdusiewicz. Reprinted by permission of the author. "Index music by Susan Burkey. • "It fell in the city" from BLACKBERRY INK by Eve Merriam. Copyright © 1985 by Eve Merriam. Reprinted by permission of Marian Reiner. • "Just Watch" from WHISPERS AND OTHER POEMS by Myra Cohn Livingston. © 1958 by Myra Cohn Livingston. © Renewed 1986 Myra Cohn Livingston. Reprinted by permission of Marian Reiner for the author. • "Keziah" from BRONZEVILLE BOYS AND GIRLS by Gwendolyn Brooks. Copyright © 1956 by Gwendolyn Brooks Blakely. Selection reprinted by permission of HarperCollins Publishers. • "Lady bug, Lady bug" from CHINESE MOTHER GOOSE RHYMES selected & edited by Robert Wyndham, copyright © 1968 by Robert Wyndham. Reprinted by permission of Philomel Books. • "Little Seeds" from THE WINDS THAT COME FROM FAR AWAY by Else Holmelund Minarik. Text copyright © 1964 by Else Holmelund Minarik. Selection reprinted by permission of HarperCollins Publishers. • "Look at Me!" © 1991 by Babs Bell

Hajdusiewicz. Reprinted by permission of the author. • "Looking Glass" by Leland B. Jacobs. Reprinted by permission of Allan Jacobs. • "Maytime Magic" by Mabel Watts. Reprinted by permission of Patricia Linda Babcock for the author. • "Merry-Go-Round" from I LIKE MACHINERY by Dorothy Baruch. Reprinted by permission of Bertha Klausner International Literary Agency, Inc. • "Mixed-Up Me" by Wilma Yeo. Used by permission of the author. • "Moochie " from HONEY, I LOVE by Eloise Greenfield. Text copyright © 1978 by Eloise Greenfield. Selection reprinted by permission of HarperCollins Publishers. • "Morning Exercises" © 1992 by Babs Bell Hajdusiewicz. Used by permission of the author. Music by Janet Cubic Sima. •"Mr. Bear" © 1987 and "My Bones" © 1991 by Babs Bell Hajdusiewicz. Used by permission of the author. "My Bones" Melody by Babs Bell Hajdusiewicz. Accompaniment by Janet Cubic Sima. • "Mr. Frog is Full of Hops" by John W. Schaum. Copyright © 1945 BELWIN-MILLS PUBLISHING CORP. c/o CPP/BELWIN, INC., Miami, FL 33014 International Copyright Secured Made in U.S.A. All Rights Reserved • "Mud Monster" by Bonnie Kinne. Reprinted by permission of the author. • "My Faces" © 1991 by Babs Bell Hajdusiewicz. Reprinted by permission of the author. • "My Friends" lyrics by Sydnie Meltzer Kleinhenz. Music by Mike Kleinhenz. Used by permission. • "My Nipa Hut-Bahay Kubo" English translation by Olcutt Sanders. Permission granted by World Around Songs. • "My True Story" © 1991 by Babs Bell Hajdusiewicz. Reprinted by permission of the author. • "New Baby" by Mary Carter Smith. Reprinted by permission of the author. • "Night Bear" reprinted by permission of Curtis Brown, Ltd. Copyright © 1972 by Lee Bennett Hopkins. • "Old Snake Has Gone to Sleep" from NIBBLE NIBBLE by Margaret Wise Brown. Text copyright © 1959 by William R. Scott, Inc. Renewed 1987 by Roberta Brown Rauch. Selection reprinted by permission of HarperCollins Publishers. • "One for Me" © 1986 by Babs Bell Hajdusiewicz. Reprinted by permission of the author. • "Our Washing Machine" reprinted with permission of Atheneum Publishers, an imprint of Macmillan Publishing Company, from THE APPLE VENDOR'S FAIR by Patricia Hubbell. Copyright 1963, and renewed 1991, by Patricia Hubbell. • "The Poet Says" © 1986 and "Poet Unknown" © 1986 and "Pop! Poppity! Pop! © 1991 by Babs Bell Hajdusiewicz. Reprinted by permission of the author. • "Polka-Dot Caterpillar" by Gail Blasser Riley. Reprinted by permission of the author.• "Rainbow Colors" © 1990 by Babs Bell Hajdusiewicz. Reprinted by permission of the author. • "Rides" by Ilo Orleans, reprinted by permission of Karen S. Solomon. • "Sand" by John Foster, first published in ANOTHER FIRST POETRY BOOK (Oxford University Press), included by permission of the author. •"Satellite" by Ollie James Robertson. Copyright © 1983 by the Instructor Publications. Reprinted by permission of Scholastic Inc. • "Satellite" by Doris Parnell Cox. Reprinted by permission of the author. • "Secret" by Beverly McLoughland. Reprinted by permission of the author who controls all rights. Originally appeared in SIDE BY SIDE, by Lee Bennett Hopkins, Simon & Schuster, 1988. • "Seeds" © 1991 by Delia Fira. Used by permission of the author. • "Shadow Me" from CLIFFORD'S SING ALONG, lyrics by Carl Tillmanns, musical arrangement by Daniel A. Burwasser. Copyright © 1987 by Scholastic Books, Inc. • "Shoes" by Rosalyn E. Figge. Reprinted by permission of the author. • "Shopping Day" © 1991 and "Skeleton's Clothes" © 1991 and "Skerbunker Doodles!"© 1992 by Babs Bell Hajdusiewicz. Reprinted by permission of the author. Musical accompaniment for "Skerbunker Doodles!" by Janet Cubic Sima. • Excerpt of "Signs" from RHYMES FOR LEARNING TIMES by Louise Binder Scott © 1983 T.S. Denison and Company Inc. Minneapolis, MN. Reprinted by permission of publisher. • "Six Speckled Hens" © 1990 by Babs Bell Hajdusiewicz. Used by permission of the author. • "Sleeping Outdoors" from Rhymes About Us by Marchette Chute. Published 1974 by E.P.

ACKNOWLEDGMENTS

Dutton. Copyright 1974 by Marchette Chute. Reprinted by permission of Elizabeth Roach. • "Sleepy Fingers" diagrams by Marc Brown from FINGER RHYMES by Marc Brown. Copyright © 1980 by Marc Brown. Used by permission of Dutton Children's Books, a division of Penguin Books USA Inc. • "Sliding" from Around and About by Marchette Chute, copyright 1957 by E.P. Dutton . Copyright renewed 1984 by Marchette Chute. Reprinted by permission of Elizabeth Roach. • "Snail" from SELECTED POEMS by Langston Hughes. Copyright 1947 by Langston Hughes. Reprinted by permission of Alfred A. Knopf, Inc. • "Sneezing" by Marie Louise Allen from LET'S ENJOY POETRY, published by Everyman's Library. Reprinted with permission. • "Sounds" by Mary Carter Smith. Reprinted by permission of the author. • "A Special Day" by Sandra Liatsos. Copyright © 1991 by Sandra Liatsos. Reprinted by permission of the author's agent, Marian Reiner. • "Special Me" © 1991 by Babs Bell Hajdusiewicz. Reprinted by permission of the author. • "Spring" by Prince Redcloud. Lee Bennett Hopkins for "Spring" by Prince Redcloud. All rights controlled. By permission of Lee Bennett Hopkins for the author. • "Stop Sign's Song" ©1991 and "Squirmy Earthworm" © 1990 by Babs Bell Hajdusiewicz. Used by permission of the author. • "Stop, Drop, and Roll" by Mary Dodson Wade. Reprinted by permission of the author. • "Streets" by Aileen Fisher. Reprinted by permission of the author. • "Subway" © 1991 and "Sun Fun" © 1990 by Babs Bell Hajdusiewicz. Reprinted by permission of the author. • "Swish, swash" from BLACKBERRY INK by Eve Merriam. Copyright © 1985 by Eve Merriam. Reprinted by permission of Marian Reiner. • "Thanksgiving" by Margaret Hillert who controls all rights. Reprinted by permission. • "Thaw" by Eunice Tietjens. Reprinted by permission of Marshall Head. • "The Berry Family" by Bonnie Kinne. Used by permission of the author. • "The Caterpillar" diagrams by Marc Brown. From HAND RHYMES by Marc Brown. Copyright © 1985 by Marc Brown. Used by permission of Dutton Children's Books, a division of Penguin Books USA Inc. • "The Frog on the Log" by Ilo Orleans. Repirnted by permission of Karen S. Solomon. • "The Funny House" by Margaret Hillert who controls all rights. Reprinted by permission. •"The Graceful Elephant" from ARROZ CON LECHE: POPULAR SONGS AND RHYMES FROM LATIN AMERICA by Lulu Delacre. Copyright © 1989 by Lulu Delacre. Reprinted by permission of Scholastic Inc. • "The Lion Roars with a Fearful Sound" by Mabel Segun. Reprinted by permission of the author. • "The north wind doth blow" Melody by Babs Bell Hajdusiewicz. Accompaniment by Janet Cubic Sima. • "The Pretty Butterfly" from TORTILLITAS PARA MAMA AND OTHER SPANISH RHYMES selected and translated by Margot C. Griego, Betsy L. Bucks, Sharon S. Gilbert, and Laurel H. Kimball. Copyright © 1981 by Margot Griego, Betsy Bucks, Sharon Gilbert and Laurel Kimball. Reprinted by permission of Henry Holt and Company, Inc. • "The Purple People Eater" © 1958 by Sheb Wooley. Used by permission of Channel Music Co. ASCAP • "The Train" translated by Mary S. de Saettone. Used by permission of World Around Songs. • "The Worried Caterpillar" by Marilyn Collett. Reprinted by permission of the author. • "This Tooth" by Lee Bennett Hopkins. Reprinted by permission of Curtis Brown, Ltd. Copyright © 1970 by Lee Bennett Hopkins. • "Thumb Says" © 1992 by Babs Bell Hajdusiewicz. Reprinted by permission of the author. • "Tiger" reprinted by permission of Gina Maccoby Literary Agency. Copyright © 1959, copyright renewed 1987 by Mary Ann Hoberman. • "To Catch a Fish" by Nanette VanWright Mellage. Reprinted by permission of the author. • "Toaster Time" from THERE IS NO RHYME FOR SILVER by Eve Merriam. Copyright © 1962, 1990 by Eve Merriam. Reprinted by permission of Marian Reiner. • "Tommy" from BRONZEVILLE BOYS AND GIRLS by Gwendolyn Brooks. Copyright © 1956 by Gwendolyn Brooks Blakely. Selection reprinted by permission of HarperCollins Publishers. • "Tower of Blocks" excerpt from "Keyboard Talent Hunt, Book 1." Reprinted by permission of Schaum Publications, Inc. copyright holder. • "Toy Tik Ka" by Charlotte Pomerantz. Reprinted by permission of Writers House Inc. • "Traffic Light" © 1991 and "Turkey Gobbler" © 1991 by Babs Bell Hajdusiewicz. Reprinted by permission of the author. • "Turtles" from Town and Countryside Poems by John Travers Moore. Copyright 1968 by John Travers Moore and published by Albert Whitman & Company. Reprinted by permission of the author. • "two friends" from SPIN A SOFT BLACK SONG by Nikki Giovanni. Copyright © 1971,1985 by Nikki Giovanni. Reprinted by permission of Farrar, Straus & Giroux, Inc. • "Two little sisters" from CHINESE MOTHER GOOSE RHYMES selected & edited by Robert Wyndham, copyright © 1968 by Robert Wyndham. Reprinted by permission of Philomel Books. • "Under Outer" © 1991 and "Vacuum" © 1991 by Babs Bell Hajdusiewicz. Reprinted by permission of the author. • "Valentine Feelings" by Lee Bennett Hopkins. Reprinted by permission of Curtis Brown, Ltd. Copyright © 1975 by Lee Bennett Hopkins. • "Walking" from I FEEL THE SAME WAY by Lilian Moore. Copyright © 1967 by Lilian Moore. Reprinted by permission of Marian Reiner for the author. • "Watching the full moon" a haiku by Basho. From CRICKET SONGS Japanese haiku translated by Harry Behn. © Renewed 1992 by Prescott Behn, Pamela Behn Adam, and Peter Behn. Used by permission of Marian Reiner. • "Wee Willie Winkie" Music by Babs Bell Hajdusiewicz. • "Whose Shoes?" © 1991 by Babs Bell Hajdusiewicz. Reprinted by permission of the author. • "What If . ." by Isabel Joshlin Glaser from GOOD BOOKS, GOOD TIMES!, compiled by Lee Bennett Hopkins, published by HarperCollins, 1990. Used by permission of the author who controls all rights. • "When I Grow Up" © 1991 and "Where's My Seat Belt?" © 1986 and "Whoooo Am I?" © 1991 by Babs Bell Hajdusiewicz. Reprinted by permission of the author. • "Who Has Seen the Wind?" words by Christina Rossetti, music by L.E. Watters from Singing Together of OUR SINGING WORLD, © 1959, 1957, 1951, by Ginn and Company. Used by permission of Silver Burdett Ginn Inc. • WILD GEESE (From CHILDREN'S SONGS FROM JAPAN) Words and Music by Florence White and Kazuo Akiyama. Copyright © 1960 by EDWARD B. MARKS MUSIC COMPANY Copyright renewed. International Copyright Secured. All Rights Reserved. Used by Permission • "Wind" (original title "Who?") from MOON-UNCLE, MOON-UNCLE: RHYMES FROM INDIA by Sylvia Cassedy and Parvathi Thampi. Reprinted by permission of Ellen Cassedy.• Text of "Winter Signs" from IT"S SNOWING, IT"S SNOWING by Jack Prelutsky. Text Copyright © 1984 by Jack Prelutsky. By permission of Greenwillow Books, a divison of William Morrow & Company, Inc. • "Wouldn't You" from YOU READ TO ME, I'LL READ TO YOU by John Ciardi. Copyright © 1962 by John Ciardi. Selection reprinted by permission of HarperCollins Publishers. • "Yes or No" © 1991 by Babs Bell Hajdusiewicz. Reprinted by permission of the author. • "Yesterday's Paper" by Mabel Watts. Reprinted by permission of Patricia Linda Babcock. • "You" from ALL THAT SUNLIGHT by Charlotte Zolotow. Text copyright © 1967 by Charlotte Zolotow. Selection reprinted by permission by HarperCollins Publishers. • "Your Shadow Says" © 1989 by J. Patrick Lewis. Reprinted by permission of the author. • "Zoo" from Town and Countryside Poems by John Travers Moore. Copyright 1968 by John Travers Moore and published by Albert Whitman & Co. Reprinted by permission of the author. •

PATTERNS

Page 18

 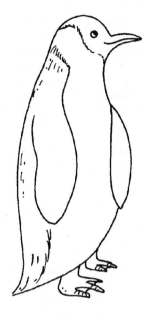 

Page 66 and 76

 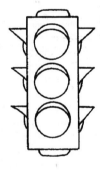 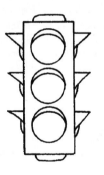 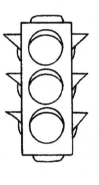 

  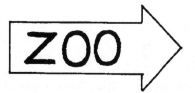

271

PATTERNS

Page 24

Page 90

Page 98

Page 96

Page 142

Page 84

272